Sainsbury's

100 Step-by-Step

Fish Dishes

Sainsbury's

100 Step-by-Step

Fish Dishes

Janette Marshall

The author

Janette Marshall is a freelance writer, specializing in cookery, food and health. Her other titles include the Sainsbury's *Vitality Cookbook* and the best-selling *Eat for Life Diet*. She is also a regular contributor to national magazines and newspapers.

Acknowledgements

A big thank you to all the tasters, testers and double testers: Tim Ball; Julie, Alan, Lindsay and James Batty; Ian and Andrea Goodall; Britt-Marie Dunn; Richard and Valerie Francis; Hilary Gould; David, Marjorie, Matthew and Rebecca Haverty; David Johnstone; Mary Lambert; Ian and Inga Marshall; Kathy Moyse; Mary and Hugh Rapley, Lydia, Sids (yes) and Alice Sidaway; Andrew Simmonds; Mitzie Wilson.

Notes

Fresh herbs are used in the recipes throughout this book unless otherwise stated.
Ingredients are given in both metric and imperial measures. Use either set of quantities but not a mixture of both in any one recipe.
All spoon measurements are level unless otherwise stated.
All eggs are standard size 3 unless otherwise stated.
Some of the recipes in this book contain raw eggs. Consumers are reminded of the advice from the Department of Health that it would be prudent for consumers, particularly those who are more vulnerable, to avoid eating raw eggs or uncooked dishes made from them. Readers are therefore advised to use their own judgement when selecting recipes.

Published exclusively for J Sainsbury plc
Stamford House, Stamford Street
London SE1 9LL
by HarperCollins*Publishers*
London

Produced by SP Creative Design
Linden House, Kings Road
Bury St Edmunds, Suffolk
Editor: Heather Thomas
Art director: Rolando Ugolini

Cover photography: David Armstrong
Cover and text design: Beverley Speight
Food preparation for cover: Roz Denny

Photographer: David Armstrong
Food preparation: Gina Steer and Dawn Stock
Step-by-step photography: Des Adams, GGS Photographics, Norwich

Project editor for HarperCollins*Publishers*: Barbara Dixon

ISBN 0583 31693 X

First published 1994

Text and photographs
© HarperCollins*Publishers* 1994

Pictured on front cover:
(*left*) Creole Fish Soup, page 15
(*right*) Grilled Halibut Steaks with Salsa Verde, page 52
Pictured on back cover: Sweet & Sour Monkfish Stir-Fry, page 68

Contents

Fish

Fish is one of the quickest and easiest foods to cook. For an increasing number of health-conscious people it has many advantages, mainly being lean and low in fat. The fat that oily fish contains is beneficial to health. You don't have to be an expert cook with special skills to enjoy fish because much of the preparation (descaling, cleaning and filleting – even the skinning and preparation of shellfish) has already been done. However, if you do want to learn these skills, this book gives instructions.

Never before has there been such a wide range of fish available all year round, thanks to quicker distribution of fresh fish and sophisticated frozen-at-sea techniques operating around the world. Fish fall into two main categories: oily or white. Oily fish includes salmon, trout, mackerel, herring, mullet, sardines and pilchards. White fish includes cod, haddock, plaice, sole, Dover sole, halibut, brill, turbot, flounder, dab, hake, whiting and sea bream. The three basic cuts of fish are fillet, steak or cutlet. Many fish are cooked whole.

Buying and storing fish

All the above fish and shellfish can be bought fresh from the wet fish counter or cold counter where they are pre-packed, or they may be bought frozen. The recipes give guidance on specific quantities, but on average allow 150-250 g (5-8 oz) per person for steaks, fillets and cutlets; and 375-500 g (12 oz-1 lb) for whole fish on the bone. Fresh fish is best used on the day it is bought, but it will store in the fridge at 4°C (40°F) for up to three days. Pre-packed fresh fish will probably keep longer (be guided by 'use by' dates on the packs) because the pack has been flushed with a mixture of gases (nitrogen, carbon dioxide and oxygen) which slows down bacterial growth.

If the fish has not been previously frozen (packs and labels on the wet fish counter will state whether this is the case), it can be frozen safely at home. Previously frozen fish is unsuitable for freezing. Gas flushing does not affect freezing quality, but obviously the best freezing results are obtained from freezing very fresh fish, which is why frozen-at-sea frozen fish is good. Freezing fish at home needs to be done carefully so that ice crystals do not form and break up the texture of the flesh. Put the booster control on the freezer to ensure it is at its coldest before introducing fish to be frozen. Thaw fish slowly (overnight) in the refrigerator to retain its texture. Fish will store for three months in a properly maintained freezer.

Buying and storing shellfish

Shellfish should also be used as soon as possible, preferably on the day that it is bought. Do not keep it in the refrigerator for more than a day. Mussels, clams and oysters should definitely be alive, with the shells shut tightly. Any that are broken or open (or do not close when put into cold salted water) should be thrown away. To store them in the refrigerator, place them in a container and cover with a cloth or teatowel soaked in cold salted water. Change the cloth after 12 hours.

Prawns can be bought uncooked but are usually sold cooked and peeled. Uncooked prawns are grey; they turn pink on cooking. Simply boil in water in a covered pan for 5 minutes, or use as instructed in the recipe.

Scallops are usually sold opened and cleaned with the intestines removed. To open, hold the shell, rounded-side uppermost, and insert a short sharp blade into the hinge muscle. Twist the blade and pull back the rounded shell. Scrape away the fringe and cut out the black intestines. Slip the blade beneath the scallop to remove it from the shell. The coral part should remain intact as it is edible – in fact, a delicacy.

Preparing fish

The recipes generally use ready-prepared fish, but should you wish to learn how to prepare fish yourself here is a resume of basic techniques. The way in which the fish is prepared, e.g. whether it is whole, cut into fillets (boneless pieces) or cut into steaks, also influences how it is best cooked.

■ **Scaling fish:** You need to do this if cooking whole fish or if using unskinned fillets. Do this over the sink or cover a flat surface with newspaper. Lay the fish down and hold it by the tail. Using a blunt knife, scrape away the scales, working from the tail towards the head. From time to time, rinse the scales off the knife under cold water.

■ **Cleaning fish:** This term is used for gutting fish. Round fish and flat fish are cleaned in different ways. For round fish, e.g. herring, mackerel and trout, slit the fish along the belly from behind the gills to just above the tail. Scrape out the entrails. Rinse the gut cavity under the cold tap and rub away any black skin. Cut off the gills below the head, and cut off the fins. If the recipe calls for headless fish, cut the head off just below the gills and slice off the tail. If you leave the head on (for grilling whole fish or barbecuing), take out the eyes.

For flat fish, e.g. plaice and sole, open the cavity containing the entrails by placing the fish, dark side up, on a flat surface and making a slit behind the gills. Scrape out the entrails and wash under a cold tap. Cut off the fins and cook the fish whole or fillet it.

■ **Skinning fish:** To skin whole round fish, make a slit in the skin around the head on one side and loosen the skin. Pull it down towards the tail where it can be cut off. Repeat for the other side.

To skin flat fish, work with the dark skin uppermost and slit above the tail. Loosen the skin, pull it towards the head and cut it off. The white skin on the other side is usually left on.

■ **Filleting fish:** For round fish, remove the head and cut along the backbone, working towards the tail and gently easing the flesh from the bone. Once the whole fillet is free, open out the fish and cut it off at the tail. Repeat for the other side.

For flat fish, place the fish, dark-skin uppermost, on a flat surface, and cut along the backbone, working from head to tail. Make a semi-circular cut below the head to the backbone, and work the knife along the bone to separate and lift the fillet off the bone. Repeat with the second fillet, turn the fish over and repeat to produce two more fillets from the other side.

■ **Boning cooked fish:** After the fish, e.g. salmon or trout, has been poached and drained, place it on a board and snip the skin below the head and above the tail. Peel off the skin, and then snip the backbone at the head and tail and insert the blade of a sharp knife along the backbone. Gently ease the bone out from the back.

Cooking fish

Oily and white fish can be cooked in a variety of ways. Oily fish are more suited to barbecuing and grilling because they have 'built-in' oils that baste the fish as it cooks. White fish are more delicate and so better suited to poaching and other methods. As a rough guide, these are the most successful cooking methods for different cuts of fish:

■ **Baking:** This is suitable for fillets, steaks and whole fish. Lay the fish in a buttered ovenproof dish. For whole fish, make about four diagonal scores through the skin on each side. Cover and bake at Gas Mark 4/180°C/350°F for approximately 10 minutes for fillets, 20 minutes for steaks, and 30 minutes for whole fish. Fillets will need regular basting, as will whole fish if they are not covered. Fish may also be baked in greaseproof paper or foil parcels to seal in juices and flavour.

■ **Frying:** This is the traditional way to cook fillets of cod and haddock and whole round fish such as herring. For shallow-frying, first dip the fish in eggwash and seasoned flour and/or breadcrumbs, and then put into hot oil or butter (or a mixture of both) and fry until golden brown, allowing about 10 minutes each side, depending on the thickness of the piece of fish. Small fish, e.g. sardines and whitebait, are usually deep-fried. To check that the oil is at the right temperature for deep-frying, drop in a 2.5 cm (1-inch) square bread cube; it should become golden brown in 1 minute. Coat the fish in a milk and flour batter before deep-frying.

■ **Grilling:** This is a low-fat cooking method, which is better for health. It is versatile and suited to fillets, steaks and whole fish. Baste white fish and fillets with olive oil and/or lemon juice during grilling. Oily fish, e.g. sardines, trout, herring and mackerel, need no basting. Preheat the grill to a high temperature and cook the fish quickly. Fillets take about five or six minutes and do not need to be turned over. Steaks take around 12 minutes and are turned half-way through cooking, as are whole fish.

■ **Poaching:** This is good for small, delicate fillets and steaks that might break up if grilled or fried. The fish is only just covered in water or stock, or a mixture of water and wine to which seasoning and herbs are added. The liquid is brought to simmering point and kept at that point until the fish is cooked. Poaching can be done in the oven or on the hob. Large fish, such as salmon and salmon trout, are usually poached whole in court bouillon (carrots, onion, celery, bay leaf, bouquet garni and white wine).

■ **Steaming:** This is probably one of the healthiest cooking methods as the fish cooks quickly, does not leach nutrients (vitamins and minerals) into the cooking liquid and no fat is added. Fillets, steaks and whole fish can be steamed over hot water, stock or court bouillon.

■ **Stir-frying:** This cooks fish and shellfish quickly, retaining the flavour. There are endless permutations of mixtures of fish and vegetables cooked with different spices and herbs.

Fish stock

This can be bought ready-made or you can make your own. You will need about 750 g (1^1/$_2$ lb) of fish bones and heads, which should be washed and trimmed and poached for 20 minutes in 1 litre (1^3/$_4$ pints) water to which you have added 10 peppercorns, 6 parsley stalks, 1 unpeeled onion and the juice of half a lemon.

Aioli

This Provençal sauce goes well with many fish dishes, especially Mediterranean fish stews and soups.

INGREDIENTS
6 garlic cloves, chopped
pinch of sea salt and ground white pepper
2 free-range egg yolks
200 ml (7 fl oz) extra-virgin olive oil
juice of 1 lemon

Using a pestle and mortar, work the garlic and seasoning together. Add the egg yolks, and then add the oil, drop by drop, until the sauce starts to thicken. At this point, start adding the oil more quickly. When half of the oil is combined, gently stir in the lemon juice. Continue blending in the rest of the oil. Adjust the seasoning before serving. Alternatively, you can make this in a food processor or blender.

CHAPTER ONE

Fish Starters

Bouillabaisse

In this classic French dish, the greater the variety of white and oily fish (not shellfish) the better it tastes. Traditionally, the broth is eaten first, followed by the fish.

Serves 4

INGREDIENTS

2 onions, chopped
2 garlic cloves, crushed
1 small fennel bulb, chopped
8 tablespoons olive oil
500 g (1 lb) tomatoes, skinned and chopped
bouquet garni (parsley stalks, bay leaf,
  sprig of thyme)
1 strip of orange zest, blanched
600 ml (1 pint) fish or vegetable stock

pinch of saffron strands, steeped in 2
  tablespoons boiling water
375 g (12 oz) white fish, e.g. whiting,
  monkfish, John Dory, haddock,
  flounder, skinned and cut into chunks
375 g (12 oz) oily fish, e.g. mackerel, red
  mullet, sardines, eel, bass, cut into pieces
sea salt and freshly ground black pepper
4 tablespoons chopped parsley, to garnish

Gently fry the onions, garlic and fennel in half of the olive oil until soft but not browned.

Add the rest of the olive oil, the saffron and its soaking water, and the fish (in the order in which they will take to cook) and bring to boiling point.

Add the tomatoes, bouquet garni, orange zest and stock and bring to the boil for 10 minutes.

Boil for about 10 minutes until the fish is cooked. Adjust the seasoning and ladle into serving dishes, ensuring that everyone gets a fair selection of fish. Sprinkle with parsley and serve with hot crusty bread.

Clam Chowder

1 onion, chopped
4 rashers unsmoked/green back bacon, chopped
2 tablespooons vegetable oil
375 g (12 oz) potatoes, chopped
450 ml (¾ pint) skimmed milk
326 g can of sweetcorn, no added salt or
sugar, drained
290 g can of clams, drained
sea salt and freshly ground black pepper
2 tablespoons chopped chives, to garnish

1 Gently fry the onion and bacon in the oil until the onion is soft but not brown. Remove a tablespoon of bacon pieces for the garnish. Stir in the potatoes and cook for a further 5 minutes.

2 Stir in the milk and continue cooking for 10 minutes, or until the potatoes are cooked. Remove from the heat and liquidize. Return to the pan and bring back to the boil.

3 Reduce the heat and add the sweetcorn and clams and simmer for 10 minutes. Adjust the seasoning and pour into serving bowls. Sprinkle with chives and bacon before serving.

Serves 4

Cream of Mussel Soup

4 shallots, chopped
1 thick celery stick, chopped
25 g (1 oz) butter
2 kg (4½ lb) mussels in their shells, scrubbed
and cleaned
300 ml (½ pint) dry white wine
600 ml (1 pint) fish or vegetable stock
bouquet garni (parsley stalks, bay leaf,
sprig of thyme)
150 ml (¼ pint) single cream
2 tablespoons chopped parsley
sea salt and freshly ground black pepper

1 Sauté the shallots and celery in the butter until softened. Add the mussels, wine, stock, bouquet garni and seasoning, and boil for 5 minutes.

2 Strain, reserving the mussels, and remove most of them from their shells. Reserve a few for the garnish. Liquidize the cooking liquid and vegetables. Stir in the cream, mussels and chopped parsley, and season to taste.

3 Reheat the soup, without boiling, and serve hot, sprinkled with more parsley if wished and garnished with the reserved mussels.

Serves 4

Creole Fish Soup

2.5 cm (1–inch) piece of fresh root ginger, grated
1 onion, chopped
1 red pepper, chopped
1 tablespoon vegetable oil
397 g can of chopped tomatoes
175 g (6 oz) spinach leaves, freshly cooked and
chopped roughly
juice of ½ lime
300 ml (½ pint) vegetable stock or water
2 red snappers, filleted and cut into
5 cm (2–inch) strips
sea salt and freshly ground black pepper

1 Gently fry the ginger, onion and red pepper in the oil for about 10 minutes, until softened.

2 Add the tomatoes, spinach, lime juice and stock, and simmer for a further 10 minutes, stirring occasionally.

3 Place the fish on the top of the soup and cover the pan so that it steams for about 5–7 minutes. Stir in the fish, season to taste, and serve immediately.

Serves 4

Thai Hot and Sour Soup

375 g (12 oz) large cooked prawns, shelled
(shells reserved)
FOR THE STOCK:
1.2 litres (2 pints) water
1 dried chilli
2 kaffir lime leaves
2.5 cm (1–inch) piece of fresh root ginger
1 blade lemon grass
1 onion, chopped
sprigs of coriander to garnish
FOR THE SOUP:
1 carrot, cut into julienne strips
juice of 1 lime
2 tablespoons coriander leaves
2 teaspoons fish sauce

1 Place the prawn shells and the stock ingredients in a saucepan. Bring to simmering point and cook for 20 minutes. Strain and reserve the liquid.

2 Put the prawns and carrot in the saucepan and return the strained stock to the pan. Bring to boiling point.

3 Stir in the lime juice and coriander leaves and bring back to simmering point. Remove from the heat and stir in the fish sauce. Ladle into serving dishes and garnish with coriander.

Serves 4

Smoked Haddock Pâté

THIS DELICIOUS SMOKY PATE MAKES AN EXCELLENT STARTER,
AND EVEN TASTES GOOD ON TOAST FOR BREAKFAST. IF LIKED, BRING TO
ROOM TEMPERATURE BEFORE SERVING.

SERVES 4

INGREDIENTS

300 g (10 oz) smoked haddock fillet
300 ml (½ pint) skimmed milk
1 bay leaf
6 peppercorns
250 g (8 oz) cottage cheese, drained and sieved
2 tablespoons chopped parsley
1 teaspoon lemon juice
freshly ground black pepper
TO GARNISH:
salad leaves and lemon wedges

---

1 Place the fish in a saucepan or an ovenproof dish and pour over the milk.

3  Drain the fish and, when it is cool enough to handle, flake it from the skin and bones into a mixing bowl.

2  Add the bay leaf and peppercorns and lightly poach, either on top of the stove or in a low oven, for 15 minutes.

4  Add the remaining ingredients and blend thoroughly, using a fork. Pot in 4 ramekin dishes, and refrigerate until ready to serve. Garnish with salad leaves and lemon wedges.

Smoked Salmon Pâté

250 g (8 oz) smoked salmon slices or pieces
250 g (8 oz) curd cheese
juice of ½ lemon
freshly ground black pepper
lemon wedges and sprigs of dill, to garnish

1 Cut the smoked salmon into strips and place in a food processor, a mortar or a sturdy bowl.

2 Add the cheese and pound or process the pâté to a smooth consistency. Fold in the lemon juice and a generous amount of freshly ground black pepper.

3 Using 2 dessertspoons, mould the pâté into egg shapes, and place 2 on each individual serving plate. Garnish with lemon wedges and sprigs of dill, and serve with brown bread and butter.

Serves 4

Smoked Mackerel Pâté

300 g (10 oz) smoked mackerel fillets
1 teaspoon ground mace
50 g (2 oz) unsalted butter
100 g (3½ oz) low–fat soft cheese (curd or quarg or sieved cottage cheese)
juice and grated zest of ½ lemon
freshly ground black pepper
lemon slices and sprigs of parsley, to garnish
pitta bread and vegtable crudités, to serve

1 Flake the fish from the skin and bones (if necessary) and mix with the mace. Place in a food processor.

2 Beat the butter to soften it and add to the mackerel with the cheese, lemon juice and zest. Blend and season to taste with black pepper.

3 Place in a serving dish and garnish with lemon slices and parsley. Serve with pitta bread and a selection of crudités (sliced raw vegetables).

Serves 4

Fresh Salmon Terrine

250 g (8 oz) tail piece of salmon, filleted and skinned
1 bay leaf
6 peppercorns
125 ml (4 fl oz) dry white wine
2 free-range eggs, hard-boiled and chopped
flesh of 2 lemons, chopped
1 tablespoon fresh green peppercorns
2 tablespoons chopped parsley
1 red pepper, seeded, roasted and chopped
2 shallots, chopped
3 teaspoons gelatine dissolved in salmon cooking
liquid and hot fish stock or court bouillon to make up
to 300 ml (½ pint)

1 Put the salmon, bay leaf and peppercorns in the wine with enough water added to cover. Bring to simmering point and, when the fish is cooked (about 15 minutes), remove from the heat.

2 Reserve the fish stock and flake the fish. Mix with the other ingredients, except the fish stock and gelatine, and place in a terrine measuring 10 x 17.5 cm (4 x 7½ inches).

3 Pour over the gelatine and stock and leave until cold. Place in the refrigerator to set. Serve sliced.

Serves 4

Smoked Trout Pâté

1 large smoked trout
100 g (3½ oz) unsalted butter, melted
2 tablespoons mayonnaise
juice and grated zest of ½ lemon
freshly ground black pepper
2 tablespoons chopped mixed fresh herbs
flat-leaf parsley, to garnish

1 Remove the skin and bones from the trout and place the flesh in a food processor or blender.

2 Add the melted butter, mayonnaise, lemon juice and zest. Season well and blend to a smooth consistency. Stir in the pepper and herbs.

3 Place the pâté in a serving dish or ramekins and chill for 2 hours in the refrigerator. Garnish with flat-leaf parsley, and serve with bread or wholemeal toast.

Serves 4

Gravad Lax with Mustard Sauce

MARINATED FISH IS GAINING IN POPULARITY AND IS EASY TO PREPARE. THIS IS THE SWEETER OF THE TWO RECIPES FOR GRAVAD LAX IN THIS BOOK. SERVE IT WITH A SELECTION OF BREADS.

SERVES 4

INGREDIENTS

500 g (1 lb) tail piece or middle cut of salmon

FOR THE MARINADE:
25 g (1 oz) sea salt
25 g (1 oz) demerara sugar
10 black peppercorns, crushed
2 tablespoons chopped dill

FOR THE MUSTARD SAUCE:
2 tablespoons Dijon mustard
½ tablespoon light muscovado sugar
1 free–range egg yolk
6 tablespoons olive oil
1 tablespoon white wine vinegar

1

Fillet the salmon tail pieces along the backbone and remove the smaller bones, using a pair of tweezers if necessary.

3

Cover, place a weight on top and refrigerate for 2 days, turning once a day. Discard the peppercorns and dill and slice the salmon thinly.

2

Lay one piece of fish on a dish, skin-side down, and cover with the marinade ingredients. Place the second piece of salmon on top with the thick part lying on top of the thin part of the bottom half.

4

Beat the mustard, sugar and egg yolk together until smooth, and gradually drizzle in the oil, mixing thoroughly between additions. Fold in the vinegar and serve with the salmon.

Marinated Swedish Herring

6 herring fillets
25 g (1 oz) sea salt
300 ml (½ pint) water
4 shallots, diced
1 carrot, diced
flat–leaf parsley, to garnish

FOR THE VINEGAR SOLUTION:
1 teaspoon whole allspice
1 teaspoon black peppercorns
1 teaspoon white mustard seeds
1 bay leaf
300 ml (½ pint) white wine vinegar
5 tablespoons water
2 teaspoons Demerara sugar

1 Place the fish in a shallow dish. Sprinkle with salt and add the water. Cover and leave overnight in the refrigerator.

2 The following day, rinse and pat dry on kitchen paper and cut into 2.5 cm (1-inch) pieces. Layer the fish and vegetables (shallots and carrot) in a 1.25 kg/1.2 litre (3 lb/2 pint) Kilner jar.

3 Mix together the ingredients for the vinegar solution and add to the jar. Move a skewer round in the jar to distribute the seasoning evenly. Store in the refrigerator for a week before use. This keeps well for 2 weeks.

Serves 8

Gravad Lax with Mayonnaise

500 g (1 lb) tail piece or middle cut of salmon

FOR THE MARINADE:
25 g (1 oz) sea salt
50 g (2 oz) granulated sugar
10 white peppercorns, crushed
10 mustard seeds, crushed
2 tablespoons brandy
2 tablespoons chopped dill

FOR THE DILL MAYONNAISE:
2 free–range egg yolks
1 teaspoon Dijon mustard
300 ml (½ pint) olive oil
1 teaspoon lemon juice
1 tablespoon white wine vinegar
2 tablespoons chopped dill
sea salt and freshly ground black pepper

1 Proceed as for steps1, 2 and 3 of Gravad Lax with Mustard Sauce (page 20).

2 Beat the egg yolks with the mustard and add the oil, drop by drop, beating between additions to make a thick mixture.

3 When half of the oil is incorporated, beat in half the lemon juice. Continue adding the oil, alternating with vinegar and lemon juice. Stir in the dill and season. Serve with the gravad lax.

Serves 4

Sushi-style Fish

125 g (4 oz) white short–grain rice
2 tablespoons Japanese rice vinegar or white wine
vinegar
1 teaspoon clear honey
½ teaspoon grated lemon zest
10 cm (4–inch) piece of mooli (white radish),
grated finely
125 g (4 oz) smoked salmon
sea salt and freshly ground black pepper
sliced carrot and chives, to garnish

1 Boil the rice in twice its volume of water until slightly sticky. While warm, stir in the vinegar and honey, seasoning, lemon zest and mooli. Allow to cool.

2 Form the rice into 12 rectangles, 3.75 cm long x 2.5 cm wide x 1.25 cm deep (1½ inches long x 1 inch wide x ½ inch deep), and place on a large flat serving dish.

3 Cut strips of salmon slightly larger than the top of the rice rectangles and drape them over. Serve garnished with carrots and chives.

Serves 4

Salmon Ceviche

500 g (1 lb) salmon, cut into small thin strips
1 shallot, chopped
juice of 2 lemons
1 tablespoon extra–virgin olive oil
pinch of chilli powder (cayenne)
1½ tablespoons chopped dill
sea salt and freshly ground black pepper
sliced red pepper and sprigs of dill, to garnish

1 Place the salmon, shallot, lemon juice, oil and chilli powder in a covered dish in the refrigerator for 6 hours, stirring twice.

2 Remove the salmon mixture from the refrigerator and stir in ½ tablespoon of the chopped dill. Season to taste.

3 Arrange on a serving dish and sprinkle with the remaining dill. Garnish with sliced red pepper and sprigs of dill, and serve with brown bread and butter.

Serves 4

Bagna Cauda

BAGNA CAUDA MEANS 'WARM BATH'. THIS IS A WARM
ANCHOVY DIP FROM PIEDMONT IN NORTHERN ITALY, WHICH IS SERVED
WITH COLOURFUL FRESH VEGETABLE CRUDITES.

SERVES *4*

INGREDIENTS

150 ml (¼ pint) olive oil
25 g (1 oz) unsalted butter
50 g (2 oz) anchovies, drained and chopped
2 garlic cloves, crushed
50 g (2 oz) ground walnuts
50 g (2 oz) fine fresh white breadcrumbs
TO SERVE:
vegetable crudités, e.g. celery, peppers, cucumber, radicchio, chicory, carrots

1

Put the olive oil and butter in a saucepan over low heat until the butter has melted. Stir well to combine.

3

Remove from the heat and add the breadcrumbs. Stir well and place in a dish over a source of heat to keep warm.

2

Add the anchovies, garlic and walnuts and continue to cook over low heat for 5 minutes.

4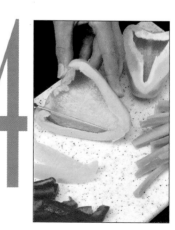

Wash and trim or slice a selection of vegetables and arrange on a dish. Offer with the bagna cauda.

Prawn and Tzaziki Dip

125 g (4 oz) peeled cooked prawns
150 ml (¼ pint) natural yogurt
¼ cucumber, chopped
4 tablespoons chopped mint
8 mini pitta breads
sliced peppers, to garnish

1 Place the prawns on a chopping board and chop them finely, or process in a food processor.

2 Transfer the chopped prawns to a bowl, and stir in the yogurt, cucumber and mint.

3 Either spoon the dip into a serving dish and offer separately with warmed mini pitta breads, or fill the pittas just before serving. Garnish with sliced peppers

Serves 4

Taramasalata

125 g (4 oz) smoked natural (undyed) cod's roe
150 ml (¼ pint) olive oil
50 g (2 oz) fine fresh white breadcrumbs
1 garlic clove, crushed
juice of 1 lemon

FOR THE GARNISH:
freshly ground black pepper
olive oil
grated lemon zest OR chopped parsley and olives

1 Skin the cod's roe and place in a food processor or liquidizer.

2 Add the remaining ingredients and blend to a smooth dip. Remove from the food processor and spoon into a serving dish.

3 Just before serving, grind some pepper over the taramasalata and drizzle over a little olive oil. Sprinkle with grated lemon zest.

Serves 4

Fresh (Lower Fat) Taramasalata

150 g (5 oz) smoked natural (undyed) cod's roe
150 ml (¼ pint) natural yogurt
50 g (2 oz) fine fresh white breadcrumbs
1 garlic clove, crushed
juice of 1 lemon
FOR THE GARNISH:
whole leaves of flat–leaf parsley
black olives
selection of crudités, e.g. broccoli and cauliflower
florets and radishes

1 Skin the cod's roe and place in a food processor or liquidizer.

2 Add the remaining ingredients and blend until smooth. Remove from the food processor and spoon into a serving dish.

3 Just before serving, decorate the top of the taramasalata with parsley and black olives. Serve with a selection of crudités.

Serves 4

Smoked Salmon and Avocado Dip

125 g (4 oz) Philadelphia cream cheese
75 g (3 oz) thick–set or greek–style natural yogurt
125 g (4 oz) smoked salmon pieces
2 tablespoons lemon juice
freshly ground black pepper
1 large ripe avocado
chopped chives and lemon slices, to garnish

1 Blend the cheese and yogurt in a food processor or blender. Add the salmon and blend until thick and smooth.

2 Remove from the blender and gradually beat in the lemon juice by hand. Season generously with black pepper. Place in a piping bag with a plain nozzle.

3 Peel the avocado and remove the stone. Cut into quarters and slice through each quarter so that it fans out. Carefully pipe the salmon mixture onto 4 serving plates, and top with the avocado fans. Sprinkle with chopped chives and garnish with lemon slices.

Serves 4

Prawn Cocktail

THIS CLASSIC AMERICAN PRAWN COCKTAIL IS SERVED WITH MARIE ROSE SAUCE. HOWEVER, THERE ARE MANY VARIATIONS ON THIS THEME, AS SHOWN IN THE RECIPES OVERLEAF.

SERVES 4

INGREDIENTS

125 ml (4 fl oz) tomato ketchup
4 tablespoons mayonnaise
1 teaspoon grated lemon zest
few drops of Tabasco (hot pepper) sauce
1 heart of a large crispy lettuce, shredded
finely

250 g (8 oz) peeled cooked prawns
FOR THE GARNISH:
lemon wedges
8 prawns in their shells
grated lemon zest

1 Blend the tomato ketchup and mayonnaise, and add the grated lemon zest and Tabasco.

3 Mix the prawns into the sauce and place on top of the lettuce.

2 Shred the lettuce and arrange, in 4 equal portions, on 4 serving dishes.

4 Garnish with lemon wedges and the prawns in their shells. Sprinkle with lemon zest. Chill and then serve with slices of brown bread and butter.

Warm Chinese Prawn Cocktail

1 tablespoon vegetable oil
1 clove garlic, crushed
1 teaspoon grated root ginger
4 spring onions, chopped
500 g (1 lb) peeled cooked prawns, minced (by
hand or in a food processor)
2 tablespoons light soy sauce
8 outer leaves from a cabbage or Chinese leaves,
blanched and thick stems removed

1 Heat the oil in a wok or frying pan and stir-fry the
garlic and ginger, without browning, for 2 minutes.
Add the spring onions, prawns and soy sauce, and
continue to stir-fry for a further 2 minutes.

2 Place a dessertspoonful of the prawn mixture on
each cabbage or Chinese leaf and wrap it up to
make a parcel.

3 Steam the parcels for about 5 minutes and serve at
once. Offer soy sauce separately.

Serves 4

Thai Prawn Cocktail

50 g (2 oz) creamed coconut, grated
2 tablespoons hot water
150 ml (¼ pint) natural yogurt
juice of ½ lime
pinch of chilli powder (cayenne)
3 spring onions, chopped
250 g (8 oz) peeled cooked prawns

FOR THE GARNISH:
1 heart of a large crispy lettuce or flowering
cabbage, shredded finely
1 mango, peeled, stoned and sliced
coarsely grated fresh coconut OR coriander

1 Mix the coconut and water in a bowl. When cool,
stir in the yogurt, lime juice and chilli powder.

2 Stir the spring onions and prawns into the dressing,
or serve the prawns separately if preferred.

3 Arrange the lettuce or cabbage leaves on 4
individual serving plates. Serve with the prawns in
their dressing, or the dip separately, and decorate
with mango slices and coconut or coriander.

Serves 4

Indian Prawn Cocktail

250 g (8 oz) peeled cooked prawns
1 tablespoon olive oil
1 garlic clove, crushed
1 green chilli, seeded and chopped finely
pinch of chilli powder (cayenne)
2 teaspoons tomato purée
2 rounded tablespoons mayonnaise
1 red pepper, seeded and chopped finely
1 heart of a large crispy lettuce, shredded finely
1 small bag of young spinach leaves, shredded finely
chilli powder (cayenne), to garnish
poppadums, to serve

1 Marinate the prawns in the oil, garlic, chilli and chilli powder overnight. Next day, fry gently for 10 minutes. Place on one side to cool.

2 Mix the tomato purée into the mayonnaise. When the prawns are cold, stir them, together with the red pepper, into the mayonnaise.

3 Arrange the lettuce and spinach in 4 equal portions, on 4 serving dishes. Place the prawn mixture on top and sprinkle each one with a small pinch of chilli powder. Serve with plain poppadums.

Serves 4

Caribbean Prawn Cocktail

1 tablespoon vegetable oil
1 green pepper, chopped finely
2 celery sticks, chopped finely
1 small onion, chopped finely
2 tomatoes, skinned and chopped
1 tablespoon chopped oregano leaves
few drops of Tabasco (hot pepper) sauce
250 g (8 oz) peeled cooked prawns
1 mango, peeled, stoned and sliced
1 small pineapple, peeled and sliced
2 papayas, peeled, stoned and sliced
sprigs of oregano, to garnish

1 Heat the oil and add the green pepper, celery and onion. Cook gently until tender, about 5 minutes, stirring occasionally.

2 Add the tomatoes and oregano, and simmer gently for a further 10 minutes. Stir in the Tabasco and prawns.

3 Arrange the prawn mixture on 4 serving dishes, and garnish the cocktail with the sliced mango, pineapple, papayas and srigs of oregano.

Serves 4

CHAPTER TWO

Shellfish

Sesame Prawn Toast

THIS VERSION OF THE CLASSIC CHINESE STARTER IS OVEN-BAKED RATHER THAN DEEP-FRIED. PREPARE THE TOASTS AS CLOSE TO EATING AS POSSIBLE TO ENSURE THAT THEY STAY CRISP.

SERVES 4

INGREDIENTS

500 g (1 lb) peeled cooked prawns, defrosted if frozen
1 tablespoon light soy sauce
2 teaspoons tomato purée
1 tablespoon white wine vinegar OR sherry vinegar
8 slices medium–thick brown bread, crusts removed
4 tablespoons sesame seeds
spring onions, to garnish

1 Preheat the oven to Gas Mark 4/ 180 °C/350 °F. Place the prawns on a chopping board and chop very finely. Transfer to a mixing bowl, and stir in the soy sauce, tomato purée and vinegar.

3 Spread the prawn mixture over the toasted bread. Top with the sesame seeds, pressing down lightly to secure in place.

2 Lightly toast the bread on both sides and place on an oiled baking sheet. Lightly toast the sesame seeds in a dry frying pan, stirring over medium heat.

4 Bake for 10 minutes until golden on top. Remove from the oven and slide on to a bread board. Slice each sesame toast diagonally and serve at once, garnished with spring onions.

Spicy Prawns on Toast

1 onion, diced
1 garlic clove, crushed
2.5 cm (1–inch) piece of fresh root ginger, peeled and grated
2 tablespoons olive oil
pinch of chilli powder (cayenne)
375 g (12 oz) tomatoes, skinned and chopped
250 g (8 oz) peeled cooked prawns
8 slices sun–dried tomato bread

1 Gently fry the onion, garlic and ginger in half of the oil in a covered pan until softened. Stir in the chilli powder.

2 Add the tomatoes and cook for 10 minutes, breaking them up with a spoon and stirring occasionally. Stir in the prawns and cook for a further 5 minutes.

3 Toast the bread and brush with the remaining oil. Top with the prawn mixture and serve immediately.

Serves 4

Prawn and Smoked Salmon Bagel

4 plain bagels
250 g (8 oz) cream or curd cheese
125 g (4 oz) peeled cooked prawns, chopped
1 tablespoon chopped dill
125 g (4 oz) smoked salmon, cut into strips
freshly ground black pepper
salad leaves and lemon wedges, to garnish

1 Preheat the grill. Cut the bagels in half and toast the cut sides under the hot grill.

2 Mix the cheese and prawns with the dill, and season with black pepper. Spread on the toasted bagel halves.

3 Top with the smoked salmon, and grind over some more pepper. Arrange on individual serving plates, and serve garnished with salad leaves and lemon wedges.

Serves 4

Toasted Crab Sandwich

1 dressed crab OR 1 x 170 g can of crab in
brine, drained
2 tablespoons mayonnaise
1 tablespoon chopped chervil
2 celery sticks, chopped finely
8 slices medium–thick brown bread
sea salt and freshly ground black pepper
salad leaves and chopped spring onions, to garnish

1 Preheat the sandwich maker, if necessary. Mix the crabmeat, mayonnaise, chervil and celery in a bowl. Season to taste with salt and pepper.

2 Take 4 slices of bread and cover each with a quarter of the crab mixture. Place another slice on top and transfer to the sandwich maker, one at a time. Cook as per the manufacturer's instructions.

3 Repeat with the remaining sandwiches. There is no need to butter the bread as it will be crispy and will retain the moisture in the sandwiches. Serve garnished with salad leaves and spring onions.

Serves 4

Seafood Salad Bruschetta

400 g (13–oz) pack of frozen seafood salad
1 tablespoon chopped parsley
500 g (1 lb) yellow and red cherry tomatoes, halved
2 tablespoons chopped basil
3 tablespoons olive oil
1 plain ciabatta loaf, cut into 2.5 cm (1–inch) slices
2 tablespoons black olive pâté OR tomato, lentil
and basil pâté
sea salt and freshly ground black pepper
grilled red–skinned onions and peppers, to garnish

1 Defrost the seafood salad and allow to come to room temperature for 30 minutes before serving. Mix in the parsley.

2 Place the tomatoes in a small saucepan with the basil and olive oil and warm through. Season to taste with salt and pepper.

3 Toast the bread lightly on both sides. Spread one side of each slice of hot bread with olive pâté. Top with the tomatoes and place spoonfuls of the seafood salad on top. Season with pepper, and garnish with grilled onions and peppers.

Serves 4

Scallops in White Wine Sauce

THIS CLASSIC SHELLFISH DISH MAKES AN EXCELLENT SUPPER. IT CAN
ALSO BE MADE IN INDIVIDUAL RAMEKINS OR SCALLOP SHELLS FOR
SERVING AS A DELICIOUS FIRST COURSE.

SERVES 4

INGREDIENTS

16 medium–sized scallops, cleaned, shelled
and sliced
150 ml (¼ pint) dry white wine
1 bay leaf
bouquet garni (parsley stalks, bay leaf, sprig
of thyme)
500 g (1 lb) boiled potatoes, mashed

125 g (4 oz) brown mushrooms, sliced
50 g (2 oz) unsalted butter
1 tablespoon plain unbleached flour
1 egg yolk
150 ml (¼ pint) double cream
sea salt and freshly ground black pepper
chopped parsley, to garnish

one of the best.

Place the scallops in a saucepan with the wine, 300 ml (¹/₂ pint) water, the bay leaf and bouquet garni, and simmer for 15 minutes. Strain through a sieve, and then reduce the liquid by one-third by boiling. Reserve.

Gently fry the mushrooms in half of the butter. Remove and keep warm. Make a roux with the rest of the butter and the flour. Gradually stir in the reduced liquid. Season and remove from the heat.

Meanwhile, put the potato in a piping bag fitted with a 1.25 cm (¹/₂-inch) star nozzle, and pipe around the circumference of a 20 cm (8-inch) shallow gratin dish, or 4 serving plates, leaving a well in the centre.

Preheat the grill. Blend the egg yolk and cream and stir into the sauce, with the scallops and mushrooms. Pour into the prepared dish(es) and reheat under the grill. Serve garnished with parsley.

Nantaise Scallops

500 g (1 lb) fresh mussels in their shells, scrubbed
and cleaned (page 42)
300 ml (½ pint) dry white wine
4 shallots, chopped
25 g (1 oz) butter
8 scallops, cleaned, removed from their shells
and halved
6 tablespoons single cream
2 tablespoons chopped parsley
sea salt and freshly ground black pepper

1 Cook the mussels in the wine in a large saucepan
for about 3 minutes, until the shells open. Remove
from the heat and remove the mussels from their
shells. Strain and reserve the cooking liquid.

2 Gently fry the shallots in the butter until softened,
but not browned. Season. Add the mussels,
scallops and the liquid in which the mussels were
cooked, and simmer for 10 minutes.

3 Remove from the heat, strain the cooking liquid
into another pan and boil to reduce by half.
Remove from the heat and stir in the cream and
parsley. Pour over the fish, heat through and serve.

Serves 4

Breton Scallops

4 shallots, chopped
65 g (2½ oz) butter
12 scallops, cleaned and removed from their shells
75 g (3 oz) fresh fine white breadcrumbs
sea salt and freshly ground black pepper
chopped parsley, to garnish

1 Preheat the oven to Gas Mark 5/190°C/375°F.
Gently fry the shallots in 25 g (1 oz) of the butter
until softened, but not browned.

2 Butter a shallow gratin dish, about 15 cm (6
inches) long, using another 25 g (1 oz) of butter,
and place the shallots in the base. Season and
arrange the scallops on top.

3 Season the breadcrumbs and spread over the
scallops. Dot with the remaining butter and bake
uncovered in the middle of the oven for 25 /30
minutes. Scatter with parsley and serve.

Serves 4

Try in shells.
Button mush sliced
3 tbl. yoghurt
—"— dbl cream
2 egg yolks.
melt butter ~ mix with bcrumbs.

Italian Scallops

2 garlic cloves, crushed
2 onions, chopped finely
3 tablespoons olive oil
750 g (1½ lb) plum tomatoes, chopped
12 scallops, cleaned and removed from their shells
50 g (2 oz) pine kernels, browned
2 tablespoons chopped parsley
250 g (8 oz) tagliatelle or linguine
sea salt and freshly ground black pepper
chopped parsley, to garnish

1 Gently fry the garlic and onions in the oil until softened. Add the tomatoes and continue to cook for 15 minutes. Transfer to a food processor, or pass through a sieve, to make a smooth sauce.

2 Return the sauce to the heat and stir in the scallops, pine kernels and parsley. Simmer for 10 minutes, and season to taste.

3 Cook the pasta in plenty of lightly salted, boiling water until cooked but *al dente* (still offering some resistance to the teeth). Drain and transfer to a serving dish. Top with the scallops and serve garnished with parsley.

Serves 4

Saffron Scallops with Rice

12 medium–sized scallops, cleaned and removed from their shells
150 ml (¼ pint) dry white wine
bouquet garni (parsley stalks, bay leaf, thyme)
a generous pinch of saffron strands OR ½ teaspoon ground turmeric
8 shallots, chopped
150 g (5 oz) shiitake mushrooms, sliced
50 g (2 oz) unsalted butter
1 tablespoon plain unbleached flour
75 g (3 oz) wild rice
75 g (3 oz) brown rice
sea salt and freshly ground black pepper

1 Put the scallops in a saucepan with the wine, 300 ml (½ pint) water, bouquet garni and saffron (or turmeric), and simmer for 15 minutes. Strain and reserve the liquid.

2 Gently fry the shallots and mushrooms in the butter until softened. Stir in the flour and gradually add the reserved liquid. Simmer for 2–3 minutes. Add the scallops and season to taste. Remove from the heat.

3 Boil the wild rice in plenty of water for 40–45 minutes. Add the brown rice 30 minutes before the end of cooking. Drain and arrange on a serving dish. Pour the scallops into the centre.

Serves 4

Moules Marinière

THE FRENCH HAVE DEVISED MANY OF THE BEST MUSSEL RECIPES, AND
THIS IS PROBABLY THE SIMPLEST AND MOST DELICIOUS OF THEM ALL.
FRESH MUSSELS ARE AVAILABLE FROM SEPTEMBER THROUGH TO APRIL.

SERVES 4

INGREDIENTS

2 kg (4½ lb) fresh mussels in their shells
3 shallots, chopped
150 ml (¼ pint) dry white wine
bouquet garni (parsley stalks, bay leaf, sprig of thyme)
2 tablespoons chopped parsley
sea salt and freshly ground black pepper

1

Scrub the mussel shells clean, scrape off any barnacles and pull out the byssus threads (beards). Discard any mussels that remain open or are cracked.

3

Add the mussels and cover the pan. Cook for about 5 minutes until all the mussels have opened. Stir occasionally or shake the pan to cook all the mussels.

2

Place the shallots, wine, bouquet garni and seasoning in a large pan and bring to the boil.

4

When the mussels open, spoon them into soup bowls to serve. Discard any that do not open. Sprinkle with parsley and strain the cooking liquid over the mussels.

Moules à la Nicoise

2 kg (4½ lb) fresh mussels in their shells, scrubbed
and cleaned (page 42)
300 ml (½ pint) dry white wine
190 g (6½ –oz) jar or home–made pesto sauce
sprigs of basil, to garnish
FOR THE PESTO SAUCE:
25 g (1 oz) fresh basil leaves (stripped from stalks)
2 garlic cloves
25 g (1 oz) pine nuts
50 g (2 oz) grated parmesan cheese
4 tablespoons olive oil
sea salt and freshly ground black pepper

1 Cook the mussels in the wine in a large saucepan for about 3 minutes, until the shells open. Remove from the heat and remove the empty side of each shell. Discard any that do not open. Strain and reserve the liquid.

2 To make the pesto, put the basil, garlic, pine nuts, parmesan and half of the olive oil in a food processor and purée until smooth. Drizzle in the rest of the oil, and season to taste.

3 Preheat the grill. Spread the pesto over the mussels and spoon over a little reserved cooking liquid to moisten. Grill for 5 minutes, until the mussels are hot and the pesto bubbling. Garnish with basil.

Serves 4

Moules Pescatora

1 onion, chopped
4 rashers unsmoked/green back bacon, chopped
2 tablespooons olive oil
290 g can of clams
150 ml (¼ pint) dry white wine
397 g can of tomatoes, chopped roughly
1 kg (2 lb) fresh mussels in their shells, scrubbed
and cleaned (page 42)
sea salt and freshly ground black pepper
16 large prawns in their shells, to garnish
garlic bread, to serve

1 Gently fry the onion and bacon in the oil until the onion has softened. Stir in the clams and continue cooking for 5 minutes. Add the wine and bring to the boil to reduce by half.

2 Add the tomatoes and cook the sauce until it is further reduced and thickened.

3 Add the mussels and cover the pan. Simmer for 5 minutes until the mussels open. Season to taste and ladle into 4 soup bowls. Garnish with the prawns, and serve with hot crusty garlic bread.

Serves 4

Moules Bonne Femme

1 kg (2 lb) fresh mussels in their shells, scrubbed and
cleaned (page 42)
150 ml (¼ pint) dry white wine
1 garlic clove, crushed
1 onion, chopped
125 g (4 oz) brown mushrooms, sliced
25 g (1 oz) unsalted butter
300 ml (½ pint) fish or vegetable stock
1 bay leaf
4 tablespoons single cream
500 g (1 lb) boiled potatoes, mashed
sea salt and freshly ground black pepper
sprigs of tarragon, to garnish

1 Cook the mussels in the white wine as in step 1 of Moules à l'Américaine. Gently fry the garlic, onion and mushrooms in the butter until the onion is soft but not brown. Pour on the reserved wine and stock. Add the bay leaf and simmer for 10 minutes.

2 Strain the stock into another pan and reduce by half. Remove from the heat and stir in the cream and add the mussels. Heat gently. Season.

3 Pipe the potatoes in a deep layer around the edge of an ovenproof serving dish and spoon the mussels and sauce into the centre. Gently heat through. Serve garnished with tarragon.

Serves 4

Moules à l'Américaine

2 kg (4½ lb) fresh mussels in their shells, scrubbed
and cleaned (page 42)
300 ml (½ pint) dry white wine
2 onions, chopped
25 g (1 oz) butter
2 tablespoons olive oil
500 g (1 lb) tomatoes, chopped
sea salt and freshly ground black pepper
sprigs of parsley, to garnish

1 Cook the mussels in the wine in a large saucepan for about 3 minutes, until the shells open. Discard any mussels that do not open. Remove from the heat and take most of the mussels out of their shells. Strain and reserve the cooking liquid.

2 Gently fry the onions in the butter and oil until soft, but not brown. Add the tomatoes and continue cooking for about 15 minutes, until the mixture thickens. Season to taste.

3 Mix the shelled mussels into the tomato sauce and heat through. Place the mixture in the centre of a serving dish, decorating with the reserved mussels in their shells and sprigs of parsley.

Serves 4

CHAPTER THREE

Main Fish Courses

Mediterranean Fish Stew

THIS IS A VARIATION ON BOURRIDE, THE GARLIC FISH STEW OF
PROVENCE. FISH STEWS MADE WITH A VARIETY OF FISH AND SHELLFISH
ARE POPULAR THROUGHOUT THE MEDITERRANEAN.

SERVES 4

INGREDIENTS

2 tablespoons olive oil
1 onion, chopped
3 celery sticks, chopped
1 fennel bulb, chopped
2 garlic cloves, crushed
1 litre (1¾ pints) fish stock
bouquet garni (parsley stalks, bay leaf,
  sprig of thyme)

1 kg (2 lb) mixed fish, e.g. red snapper, grey
  mullet, squid, sea bass, whiting, monkfish,
  conger eel, filleted and cut into chunks
125 ml (4 fl oz) aioli (see page 9)
sea salt and freshly ground black pepper
chopped parsley, to garnish
1 small baguette or ciabatta loaf, sliced,
  brushed with olive oil and toasted, to serve

1 Heat the oil in a large saucepan and add the onion, celery, fennel and garlic. Cook for about 15 minutes without browning. Add the stock and bouquet garni and bring to simmering point.

3 Gently warm the aioli. Gradually whisk in the reserved hot stock, stirring until it reaches the consistency of single cream. Do not boil.

2 Add the fish and cook for 3-4 minutes. Strain the stock, reserving the vegetables and fish. Cover them and keep warm.

4 Season to taste and ladle the stock into serving bowls. Add the fish, sprinkle with chopped parsley and serve with the toasted bread.

Mediterranean Fish Stew with Polenta

1 quantity Mediterranean Fish Stew (page 48)
FOR THE POLENTA:
450 ml (¾ pint) chicken stock
150 g (5 oz) polenta or cornmeal
250 ml (8 fl oz) cold water
1 tablespoon olive oil
sea salt and freshly ground black pepper

1   Bring the chicken stock to the boil. Blend the polenta with the cold water in a bowl, and add in one go to the pan of boiling stock. Stir until the mixture boils and thickens. Reduce the heat, season with salt and pepper, and simmer for 10 minutes until very thick, stirring constantly.

2   Remove from the heat. Spoon the mixture into a lightly oiled 20 cm (8–inch) square shallow cake tin, and smooth the top. Set aside until the polenta is completely cold.

3   When the polenta is cold, cut into squares. Lightly brush the polenta with the olive oil and fry or grill for 3–4 minutes until golden. Serve with the Mediterranean Fish Stew.

Serves 4

Indian-style Coriander Fish Stew

1 garlic clove, crushed
2.5 cm (1–inch) piece of fresh root ginger, grated
1 onion, chopped
1 teaspoon ground coriander
½ teaspoon ground cumin
¼ teaspoon ground turmeric
3 tablespoons vegetable oil
3 tomatoes, skinned and chopped
50 g (2 oz) creamed coconut
300 ml (½ pint) boiling water
550 g (1 lb 2 oz) cod, cut into chunks
375 g (12 oz) mackerel fillets
250 g (8 oz) fresh spinach leaves, steamed or boiled
15 g (½ oz) chopped coriander
sea salt and freshly ground black pepper

1   Gently fry the garlic, ginger, onion and spices in the oil for 10 minutes. Add the tomatoes and cook for a further 10 minutes.

2   Dissolve the creamed coconut in the boiling water and stir into the tomato mixture. Add the fish and the spinach, and cook gently for 8 minutes.

3   Stir in the coriander and continue cooking for another 2 minutes. Season to taste.

Serves 4

Italian Fish Stew

4 tablespoons olive oil
1 large onion, chopped
3 garlic cloves, crushed
250 g (8 oz) squid, cleaned and sliced into rings
200 ml (7 fl oz) tomato juice
397 g can of chopped tomatoes
125 g (4 oz) small tortellini filled with ricotta
and spinach
500 g (1 lb) mixed fish, e.g. red snapper and grey
mullet, cleaned, scaled, filleted and sliced
sea salt and freshly ground black pepper

1 Heat half of the olive oil and gently fry the onion and garlic until transparent. Stir in the squid and cook for a further 5 minutes.

2 Add the tomato juice and tomatoes and stir in the pasta. Cover and cook for 10 minutes.

3 Stir in the slices of red snapper and grey mullet. Continue to simmer, uncovered, for 15 minutes. Season to taste and serve immediately.

Serves 4

Brittany Fish Stew

500 g (1 lb) fresh mussels in their shells, scrubbed
and cleaned (page 42)
150 ml (¼ pint) dry white wine
1 garlic clove, crushed
1 leek, washed and sliced
1 onion, chopped
25 g (1 oz) unsalted butter
250 g (8 oz) new potatoes, scrubbed and chopped
600 ml (1 pint) fish or vegetable stock
bouquet garni (parsley stalks, bay leaf, sprig
of thyme)
375 g (12 oz) monkfish, cubed
4 large scallops, cleaned, shelled and sliced
4 tablespoons single cream
sea salt and freshly ground black pepper

1 Cook the mussels in the white wine as in step 1 of Moules Pescatora (page 44). Gently cook the garlic, leek and onion in the butter until soft. Stir in the potatoes, season and cook for 3 minutes.

2 Add the stock and bouquet garni. Stir in the monkfish, scallops and mussels, and simmer for 5 minutes.

3 Strain the liquid into another pan and reduce by half by boiling. Remove from the heat and stir in the cream. Return to the pan with the fish and gently heat through.

Serves 4

Grilled Halibut Steaks with Salsa

THIS DELICIOUS COMBINATION OF SUCCULENT FISH STEAKS AND A FRESH-
TASTING SALSA IS A 'FRUITY' WAY TO ENJOY FISH. COOKING OVER A
BARBECUE ADDS A DELICIOUS CHAR-GRILLED FLAVOUR.

SERVES 4

INGREDIENTS

4 x 150 g (5-oz) halibut steaks
olive oil for basting
1 crusty loaf or ciabatta, sliced
1 bag of mixed salad leaves, to serve
250 g (8 oz) cherry tomatoes, to serve
FOR THE SALSA VERDE:
4 tablespoons extra-virgin olive oil

2 spring onions, chopped
1 garlic clove, chopped
2 shallots, chopped
5 tablespoons chopped coriander
2 green chillies, seeded and chopped
1 teaspoon clear honey
1 tablespoon balsamic vinegar

Make the salsa verde: put half of the olive oil and the remaining salsa ingredients in a food processor, and blend to a smooth purée. Refrigerate until needed.

Transfer the hot fish steaks to 4 heated serving plates, and top with the salsa verde.

Brush the fish steaks with olive oil and cook on a hot griddle for about 5 minutes each side. Move the steaks during cooking to achieve an attractive cross-hatch marking.

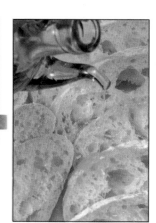

Arrange some slices of bread on each plate, and drizzle with the remaining olive oil from the salsa. Serve with salad leaves and cherry tomatoes.

Haddock Steaks
with Tapenade Crust

4 x 150 g (5–oz) haddock steaks
olive oil for basting
FOR THE TAPENADE CRUST:
2 tablespoons black olive pâté
1 garlic clove , crushed
1 tablespoon capers, drained
50 g can of anchovies, drained
1 tablespoon olive oil
sprigs of flat–leaf parsley, to garnish

1 Preheat the grill. Brush the fish steaks with olive oil and cook under the hot grill for about 5 minutes. Remove the grill pan and turn the steaks over. Set aside.

2 Put the black olive pâté, garlic, capers, anchovies and olive oil in a food processor, and blend to a smooth purée. Alternatively, work the mixture by hand, using a pestle and mortar.

3 Spread the tapenade over the uncooked side of the fish steaks, and replace the grill pan under the heat. Cook for about 5–7 minutes, until the crust is crisp and the fish cooked. Serve garnished with sprigs of parsley.

Serves 4

Salmon Steaks with Pesto Crust

4 x 150 g (5–oz) salmon steaks
olive oil for basting
FOR THE CRUST:
2 tablespoons pesto sauce (see page 44)
50 g (2 oz) very fine breadcrumbs, toasted
sprigs of basil or dill, to garnish

1 Preheat the grill. Brush the salmon steaks with olive oil, and cook under the hot grill for about 5 minutes. Remove the grill pan and turn the steaks over. Set aside.

2 Make the pesto sauce or use ready–made sauce. Stir in the breadcrumbs.

3 Spread the pesto over the uncooked side of the fish steaks and replace the grill pan under the heat. Cook for about 5–7 minutes, until the crust is crisp and the fish cooked. Transfer to 4 warm serving plates and serve garnished with basil or dill.

Serves 4

Grilled Halibut Steaks with Provencal Sauce

4 x 150 g (5–oz) halibut steaks
olive oil for basting
sprigs of oregano, to garnish
FOR THE PROVENCAL SAUCE:
6 sun–dried tomatoes in sunflower oil
1 onion, chopped
2 tablespoons oil (from the jar of tomatoes)
2 tomatoes, chopped
1 tablespoon chopped oregano or marjoram
freshly ground black pepper

1 Preheat the grill. Brush the halibut steaks with olive oil and cook under the hot grill for about 10 minutes, turning once.

2 Gently cook the sun–dried tomatoes and onion in the oil until softened. Add the tomatoes and oregano and continue cooking for about 10 minutes.

3 Remove from the heat and blend to a smooth sauce in a food processor or liquidizer. Season to taste, and place a little sauce on each serving plate. Top with the grilled fish steaks. Serve garnished with sprigs of oregano.

Serves 4

Grilled Cod Steaks with Parsley Sauce

4 x 150 g (5–oz) cod steaks
olive oil for basting
FOR THE SAUCE:
25 g (1 oz) unsalted butter
1 tablespoon plain unbleached flour
300 ml (½ pint) skimmed milk
1 teaspoon grated lemon zest
2 tablespoons chopped parsley
sea salt and freshly ground black pepper

1 Preheat the grill. Brush the cod steaks with olive oil and grill for about 10 minutes, turning once.

2 Melt the butter in a saucepan and stir in the flour to make a roux. Gradually stir in the milk until a smooth sauce is achieved. Stir in the lemon zest and parsley, and season to taste.

3 Place the cod steaks on a hot serving dish or 4 plates, and pour over the sauce. Serve with new potatoes and peas.

Serves 4

Fish Cakes

TASTY AND ECONOMICAL, FISH CAKES ARE EASY TO MAKE, ESPECIALLY IF
YOU HAVE SOME LEFT-OVER POTATO IN THE REFRIGERATOR. YOU CAN
EXPERIMENT WITH DIFFERENT FISH, AS IN THE FOLLOWING RECIPES.

SERVES 4

INGREDIENTS

250 g (8 oz) cooked cod, flaked
250 g (8 oz) cooked potato, mashed
1 tablespoon chopped parsley
1 free-range egg, beaten lightly
40 g (1½ oz) fresh white breadcrumbs
sea salt and freshly ground black pepper
vegetable oil for frying
sprigs of flat-leaf parsley, to garnish
grilled tomatoes, to serve

1  Mix the cod and potato together. Season well and stir in the parsley. Add enough egg for the mixture to hold together, and reserve some for brushing the fish cakes.

3  Brush with the reserved beaten egg and dip into the breadcrumbs.

2  When cool enough to handle, form the mixture into 4 fish cakes, using floured hands.

4  Fry the fish cakes lightly in hot oil on both sides, until golden brown. Serve hot, garnished with sprigs of parsley, with grilled tomatoes.

Salmon Fish Cakes

375 g (12 oz) cooked salmon, flaked
250 g (8 oz) waxy salad potatoes, cooked and
chopped
3 tablespoons mayonnaise
1 free–range egg, hard–boiled and chopped finely
1 tablespoon chopped parsley
1 free–range egg, beaten lightly
dry white breadcrumbs
vegetable oil for frying
sea salt and freshly ground black pepper
lemon or lime wedges and sprigs of flat–leaf parsley,
to garnish

1 Mix the salmon and potatoes together in a bowl with the mayonnaise, hard–boiled egg, parsley and some seasoning.

2 Form the mixture into 4 fish cakes. Dip each into the beaten egg and then into the breadcrumbs. Chill for 30 minutes to firm the fish cakes.

3 Lightly fry the fish cakes in hot oil for 4–5 minutes on each side, until golden. Remove from the pan and drain on absorbent kitchen paper. Serve garnished with lemon or lime wedges and parsley.

Serves 4

Thai Fish Cakes

2.5 cm (1–inch) piece of fresh root ginger, grated
1 garlic clove, crushed
2 green chillies, seeded and chopped
1 onion, chopped
2 tablespoons oil
1 dressed crab
1 teaspoon grated lime zest
pinch of ground coriander
1 free–range egg, beaten lightly
vegetable oil for frying

1 Gently fry the ginger, garlic, chillies and onion in the oil until softened but not brown. Remove from the heat.

2 Stir the crabmeat, lime zest and coriander into the cooked vegetables. Form into 8 fish cakes, using floured hands.

3 Brush with the beaten egg and fry lightly on both sides in hot oil, until golden brown.

Serves 4

Haddock and Prawn Fish Cakes

375 g (12 oz) haddock
1 bay leaf
6 peppercorns
parsley stalks
125 g (4 oz) peeled cooked prawns, chopped
250 g (8 oz) boiled potatoes, mashed
unbleached flour for coating
vegetable oil for frying
sea salt and freshly ground black pepper
salad leaves, to garnish

1 Poach the haddock in enough water to cover, with the bay leaf, peppercorns and parsley stalks. When cooked, remove the haddock from the cooking liquid and flake from the bones and skin.

2 Mix the haddock with the chopped prawns and mashed potato. Form the mixture into 4 fish cakes, using floured hands, and coat them lightly with flour.

3 Lightly fry the fish cakes in the oil for 4–5 minutes on each side until golden. Remove from the pan and drain on absorbent kitchen paper. Garnish with salad leaves.

Serves 4

Eastern Fish Cakes

375 g (12 oz) mackerel fillets, skinned
250 g (8 oz) coley fillets, skinned
1 garlic clove, crushed
1 onion, chopped
½ teaspoon ground cumin
½ teaspoon ground coriander
1 tablespoon tomato purée
vegetable oil for deep-frying
sea salt and freshly ground black pepper
lime wedges and sprigs of coriander, to garnish

1 Place the mackerel, coley, garlic, onion, cumin, coriander, tomato purée and seasoning in a blender or food processor, and purée to a smooth paste.

2 Form the mixture into 8 small balls, using floured hands. Deep-fry them in hot oil until they are cooked and golden.

3 Remove and drain on absorbent kitchen paper. Serve garnished with lime wedges and coriander.

Serves 4

Prawn Risotto

A GOOD RISOTTO SHOULD BE MOIST BUT NOT STICKY. FOR THE BEST
RESULTS, USE ITALIAN ARBORIO RISOTTO RICE. RISOTTO IS A MEAL IN
ITSELF RATHER THAN AN ACCOMPANIMENT TO A MAIN DISH.

SERVES 4

INGREDIENTS

1 tablespoon olive oil
2 celery sticks, chopped
1 onion, chopped
250 g (8 oz) risotto rice
pinch of saffron strands
175 g (6 oz) peeled cooked prawns
750 ml (1¼ pints) boiling fish or vegetable stock
3 tablespoons chopped flat-leaf parsley
sea salt and freshly ground black pepper
freshly grated parmesan cheese, to serve

1
Heat the oil in a pan and add the celery and onion, and fry gently until soft. Stir in the rice and saffron and continue stirring over moderate heat for about 5 minutes, until the rice is slightly opaque.

2
Stir in the prawns and ladle some of the stock into the pan, stirring gently. Gradually add the stock, a little at a time, when necessary. Stir the risotto often.

3
The rice should take about 20 minutes to absorb the stock. When it is cooked, remove the pan from the heat.

4
Stir in the parsley and season to taste. Serve at once, in flat soup dishes. Offer the parmesan cheese separately, if liked.

Mullet Risotto

2 celery sticks, chopped
1 Spanish onion, chopped
1 tablespoon olive oil
25 g (1 oz) butter
375 g (12 oz) risotto rice
pinch of saffron strands
6 fillets red mullet, cut into 2.5 x 1.25 cm
(1 x ½ –inch) pieces
1 litre (1¾ pints) boiling fish or vegetable stock
3 tablespoons chopped flat–leaf parsley
sea salt and freshly ground black pepper
2 tablespoons freshly grated parmesan cheese

1 Gently fry the celery and onion in the oil. Add the butter and allow to melt before stirring in the rice and saffron. Continue to stir over a moderate heat for 5 minutes, until the rice is opaque.

2 Add the fish and gradually ladle the stock into the pan, stirring gently during the 20 minutes the rice takes to absorb the stock and cook.

3 Remove the pan from the heat and stir in the parsley, seasoning and parmesan cheese.

Serves 4

Paella

4 skinless, boneless chicken thighs
2 garlic cloves, crushed
1 onion, chopped
1 tablespoon olive oil
250 g (8 oz) risotto rice
125 g (4 oz) squid, cleaned and sliced into rings
175 g (6 oz) thin green beans, sliced
pinch of saffron strands
600 ml (1 pint) fish, vegetable or chicken stock
250 g (8 oz) fresh mussels in their shells, scrubbed
and cleaned (page 42)
125 g (4 oz) prawns in their shells
sea salt and freshly ground black pepper

1 Place the chicken, garlic and onion in a paella pan or non–stick frying pan with the oil, and gently fry for about 10 minutes, turning the chicken so that it is golden all over.

2 Add the rice and squid and continue cooking for 5 minutes, until the rice starts to turn opaque. Stir in the beans and saffron and pour over the stock.

3 Add the shellfish to the rice mixture and lower the heat to a gentle simmer. Cook, without stirring, for 20–25 minutes, until the rice is cooked and the stock absorbed. Season to taste and serve.

Serves 4

Kedgeree

500 g (1 lb) Finnan haddock or smoked haddock
2 free–range eggs, hard–boiled and chopped
75 g (3 oz) raw weight long–grain brown rice, boiled
freshly grated nutmeg
1 teaspoon lemon juice
150 ml (¼ pint) single cream
25 g (1 oz) unsalted butter
sea salt and freshly ground black pepper
FOR THE GARNISH:
1 tablespoon chopped parsley
lemon wedges

1. Poach the haddock in enough water to cover. When cooked, cool and flake from the bones and skin. Preheat the oven to Gas Mark 4/180°C/350°F.

2. Mix the haddock with the chopped eggs, rice, nutmeg, seasoning and lemon juice, and place in a buttered ovenproof dish. Pour over the cream and dot with the butter.

3. Cover and bake in the oven for 25–30 minutes. Remove from the oven and serve garnished with parsley and lemon wedges.

Serves 4

Jambalaya

375 g (12 oz) herby pork sausages or Cumberland sausage
1 tablespoon vegetable oil
1 onion, chopped
2 garlic cloves, crushed
250 g (8 oz) long–grain brown rice
500 g (1 lb) tomatoes, chopped
600 ml (1 pint) boiling vegetable stock or water
few drops of Tabasco (hot pepper) sauce
2 bay leaves
200 g (7 oz) peeled cooked prawns
sea salt and freshly ground black pepper
4 cooked prawns in their shells and chopped parsley, to garnish

1. Slice the sausage(s) and put in a deep saucepan with the oil, onion, garlic and rice and cook for about 7 minutes, until the rice is opaque.

2. Add the tomatoes, stock, Tabasco and seasoning. Place the bay leaves in the centre, cover and simmer for 20 minutes.

3. Stir in the prawns and cook, uncovered, until the stock reduces. Remove the pan from the heat and stir. Transfer to a serving dish and serve garnished with the prawns in their shells and chopped parsley.

Serves 4

Fish Pie

FISH PIE MAKES A WONDERFULLY NOURISHING AND TASTY FAMILY MEAL,
WHICH CAN BE MADE IN ENDLESS COMBINATIONS TO SUIT ALL TASTES.
SOME VARIATIONS ARE SUGGESTED OVERLEAF.

SERVES 4

INGREDIENTS

500 g (1 lb) white fish of your choice
6 black peppercorns
2 bay leaves
1 garlic clove, crushed
1 large onion, chopped
1 large carrot, grated

1 tablespoon vegetable oil
230 g can of chopped tomatoes
175 g (6 oz) ready–made puff pastry,
  defrosted if frozen
beaten egg or milk, for glazing
sea salt and freshly ground black pepper

1 Preheat the oven to Gas Mark 6/ 200°C/400°F. Poach the fish for 10 minutes in enough water to cover, with the peppercorns and bay leaves.

3 Gently fry the garlic, onion and carrot in the oil until soft. Add to the pie dish. Pour over the tomatoes, season and stir well.

2 When cooked and cool enough to handle, flake the fish into a 20 cm (8-inch) pie dish.

4 Roll out the pastry and cut a strip to put around the edge of the pie dish. Brush with beaten egg or milk and secure the lid in place. Glaze with beaten egg and bake for 30 minutes until well risen and golden.

- Haddock/Cod.
- Salmon.
- Prawns.
- milk / 4 shallots
- Poach fish in above.
- Remove.
- Make poaching milk into cheese sau
- Fish into pieces
- Into dish
- mash on top
- extra shredded cheese on
- top of pot. topping.
- ½ hr. in oven. 180°

Potato and Olive Oil Fish Pie

ingredients as for Fish Pie (page 64), omitting the
tomatoes and adding 125 g (4 oz) mushrooms and
125 g (4 oz) cooked frozen peas

FOR THE TOPPING:
500 g (1 lb) boiled potatoes, drained
2 garlic cloves, crushed
100 ml (3½ fl oz) olive oil
2 teaspoons lemon juice
sea salt and freshly ground black pepper

1 Make the filling as for Fish Pie steps 1, 2 and 3.
Add the mushrooms with the garlic in Step 3, and
then add the peas to the pie filling.

2 Put the potatoes, garlic, olive oil and lemon juice in
a food processor and blend to a smooth purée.
Alternatively, mash by hand. Season to taste and
pipe or spread over the top of the fish.

3 Bake for 25 minutes in the preheated oven until
heated through and golden on top.

Serves 4

Fish and Cheese Crumble

500 g (1 lb) white fish of your choice
6 black peppercorns
2 bay leaves
1 tablespoon vegetable oil
1 large onion, chopped
125 g (4 oz) mushrooms
25 g (1 oz) butter
25 g (1 oz) plain unbleached flour
150 ml (¼ pint) skimmed milk
125 g (4 oz) grated Cheddar cheese
1 tablespoon chopped parsley

FOR THE CRUMBLE TOPPING:
75 g (3 oz) plain unbleached flour
40 g (1½ oz) soft margarine

1 Cook the fish and vegetables as in Steps 1, 2 and
3 of Fish Pie (page 64), but strain and reserve the
cooking liquid. Make a roux with the butter and
flour. Gradually stir in the milk and 150 ml
(¼ pint) of the reserved cooking liquid.

2 Remove the sauce from the heat and stir in half of
the cheese. Pour over the fish in a pie dish, add the
parsley and mix well.

3 Sift the flour into a mixing bowl, rub in the fat and
stir in the remaining cheese. Sprinkle over the fish
and bake for 30 minutes.

Serves 4

Potato Fish Pie

500 g (1 lb) potatoes
25 g (1 oz) butter
4 rashers unsmoked back bacon, chopped
1 large onion, chopped
375 g (12 oz) monkfish, cubed
500 g (1 lb) cherry tomatoes, halved
freshly ground black pepper

1 Boil the potatoes and mash well with the butter. Place in a piping bag with a 1.25 cm (½–inch) star nozzle.

2 Gently fry the bacon and onion in a non–stick frying pan (there is no need to add fat). When the onion is softened, but not brown, stir in the fish and tomatoes. Season with pepper.

3 Place the fish mixture in a lightly oiled 20 cm (8–inch) round pie dish. Pipe the potato on top and bake in a preheated oven at Gas Mark 5/ 190°C/375°F for 25 minutes until the potato topping is golden.

Serves 4

Lattice Ocean Pie

1 tablespoon plain unbleached flour
25 g (1 oz) butter or soft margarine
300 ml (½ pint) skimmed milk
250 g (8 oz) coley fillet, cubed
250 g (8 oz) cod fillet, cut into strips
2 tablespoons chopped parsley
250 g (8 oz) mushrooms, sliced and fried
175 g (6 oz) ready–made shortcrust pastry
beaten egg or milk, for glazing
sea salt and freshly ground black pepper

1 Preheat the oven to Gas Mark 6/200°C/400°F. Make a roux with the flour and fat. Gradually stir in the milk to make a smooth sauce. Stir in the fish, parsley, seasoning and mushrooms.

2 Place the fish mixture in a 20 cm (8–inch) pie dish, and oil the edge of the dish. Roll out the pastry on a lightly floured board, and cut a strip to fit around the edge of the dish.

3 Press the strip into place. Roll a lattice cutter over the pastry lid and lift into position, pressing the edges into the strip already on the dish (or cut into strips and arrange in a lattice pattern over the pie). Brush with beaten egg or milk and bake for 20–25 minutes.

Serves 4

Sweet and Sour Monkfish Stir-fry

MONKFISH IS AN EXCELLENT FISH FOR STIR-FRIES AND OTHER DISHES, SUCH AS KEBABS. ITS FIRM TEXTURE GIVES A MEATY EFFECT AND IT DOES NOT FLAKE OR FALL APART WHEN COOKED.

SERVES 4

INGREDIENTS

2 tablespoons sesame oil
1 garlic clove, crushed
2.5 cm (1–inch) piece of fresh root ginger, grated
1 carrot, cut into matchsticks
1 onion, sliced
125 g (4 oz) broccoli florets
1 red pepper, seeded and cut into strips
150 g (5 oz) mange tout, trimmed

425 g (14 oz) monkfish, boned and cubed
FOR THE SAUCE:
3 tablespoons soy sauce
juice of 1 orange
2 teaspoons tomato purée
1 tablespoon white wine vinegar
1 tablespoon demerara sugar
2 teaspoons cornflour mixed with 4 tablespoons cold water

1 Heat all the sauce ingredients over moderate heat, stirring constantly until thickened.

2 Heat the oil in a wok or frying pan and stir-fry the garlic and vegetables, cooking them as listed in order of hardness, until cooked but not soft.

3 Add the monkfish about 3-4 minutes before all the vegetables are ready, and cook through gently.

4 Either pour the sauce over the stir-fried mixture and heat through before serving, or serve the sauce separately.

Stir-fried Crab Balls

1 dressed crab
1 teaspoon freshly grated ginger
1 garlic clove, crushed
1 tablespoon tomato purée
1 free—range egg, beaten
1 tablespoon plain unbleached flour, seasoned
2 tablespoons vegetable oil
fried vermicelli, to serve
FOR THE STIR—FRIED VEGETABLES:
1 head of broccoli, cut into florets
1 large carrot, peeled and cut into strips
1 onion, sliced
1 large courgette, cut into slices and strips
4 Chinese leaves, shredded
2 large handfuls of bean sprouts

1 Put the crabmeat in a bowl, and stir in the ginger, garlic and tomato purée. Roll into 8 balls, using floured hands. Dip each ball in the beaten egg and roll in the flour.

2 Heat the oil in a wok or frying pan and stir–fry the balls for 8–10 minutes, until golden and cooked through.

3 Stir–fry the vegetables, cooking them as listed in order of hardness, until cooked but not soft. Serve with the crab balls on a bed of fried vermicelli.

Serves 4

Scallop Stir-fry

4 tablespoons vegetable oil
1 garlic clove, crushed
2 celery sticks, sliced
1 carrot, cut into matchsticks
1 green pepper, seeded and sliced
1 blade of lemon grass, chopped
8 medium—sized scallops, cleaned, shelled and cut into thick slices
6 spring onions, chopped
6 large Chinese leaves, sliced
125 g (4 oz) black bean sauce
juice of 1 lemon

1 Heat the oil in a wok or large frying pan and gently stir–fry the garlic for 2 minutes to flavour the oil.

2 Increase the heat and add the celery, carrot, green pepper and lemon grass, and stir–fry for 2 minutes. Add the scallops, spring onions and Chinese leaves, and cook for a further 3 minutes.

3 Stir in the black bean sauce and lemon juice and heat through. Serve immediately.

Serves 4

Squid Stir-fry

750 g (1½ lb) squid, cleaned, defrosted if frozen
2 tablespoons oil
2 garlic cloves, crushed
1 red–skinned onion, sliced
1 red pepper, sliced
1 green pepper, cut into strips
3 courgettes, half cut into rounds, half into strips
2 tablespoons light soy sauce
1 tablespoon sherry
1 teaspoon tomato purée
juice of ½ lemon

1 Blanch the squid for 2 minutes in boiling water. Drain. Heat the oil in a wok or large frying pan and gently stir–fry the squid, garlic, onion and peppers for 4 minutes.

2 Add the courgettes and cook for a further 2 minutes.

3 Mix together the soy sauce, sherry, tomato purée and lemon juice, and pour over the stir–fried mixture. Turn up the heat and stir well for a further minute before serving.

Serves 4

Prawn Stir-fry

2 tablespoons sesame oil
1 garlic clove, crushed
2.5 cm (1–inch) piece of fresh root ginger, grated
125 g (4 oz) canned water chestnuts, drained and sliced
1 carrot, cut into matchsticks
6 spring onions, chopped
125 g (4 oz) mange tout, trimmed
250 g (8 oz) peeled cooked prawns

FOR THE SAUCE:
3 tablespoons soy sauce
juice of 1 orange
2 teaspoons tomato purée
1 tablespoon white wine vinegar
1 tablespoon demerara sugar
2 teaspoons cornflour mixed with 4 tablespoons cold water

1 Heat all the sauce ingredients in a saucepan over moderate heat, stirring constantly until thickened.

2 Heat the oil in a wok or frying pan and stir–fry the garlic and ginger for 3 minutes. Add the water chestnuts and carrot, and cook for 2 minutes.

3 Add the spring onions, mange tout and prawns, and cook for a further 3 minutes. Pour over the sauce and heat through.

Serves 4

Sole Véronique

THIS DISH WORKS EQUALLY WELL WITH DOVER SOLE OR LEMON SOLE. YOU CAN ALSO USE PLAICE WHICH IS A CHEAPER ALTERNATIVE TO SOLE. THE CREAMY SAUCE MAKES IT IDEAL FOR ENTERTAINING.

SERVES 4

INGREDIENTS

8 fillets of sole
2 shallots, diced
4 button mushrooms, sliced thinly
1 tablespoon chopped parsley
1 bay leaf
2 teaspoons lemon juice
150 ml (¼ pint) dry white wine

25 g (1 oz) unsalted butter
2 tablespoons plain unbleached flour
150 ml (¼ pint) milk
175 g (6 oz) seedless white grapes, skinned
sea salt and freshly ground black pepper
sprigs of dill, to garnish

Yes

Preheat the oven to Gas Mark 4/ 180°C/350°F. *160 fan* Place the fish in a 25 cm (10-inch) square ovenproof dish, and sprinkle over the shallots, mushrooms, parsley, bay leaf, lemon juice and wine.

Melt the butter in a separate pan and stir in the flour. Make the reduced liquid up to 300 ml (½ pint) with the milk. Gradually add it to the roux, stirring continuously.

Cover and bake for 15 minutes. Keep the fillets warm while you strain the liquid into a small saucepan and reduce by half.

Remove from the heat, stir in the grapes and adjust the seasoning. Fold the fillets in half on a serving dish and pour over the sauce. Garnish with sprigs of dill.

Sole Baked in White Wine Sauce

40 g (1½ oz) butter
3 carrots, sliced
1 onion, chopped
300 ml (½ pint) dry white wine
bouquet garni (parsley stalks, bay leaf, thyme)
4 Dover soles or lemon soles, cleaned and skinned
6 black peppercorns
1 bay leaf
150 ml (¼ pint) water
25 g (1 oz) plain unbleached flour
sea salt and freshly ground black pepper
chopped parsley, to garnish

1 Preheat the oven to Gas Mark 4/180°C/350°F. Melt half of the butter and gently fry the carrots and onion. Season and add half of the wine and the bouquet garni. Simmer for 15 minutes. Drain and reserve the cooking liquid.

2 Place the fish, peppercorns and bay leaf in an ovenproof dish with the rest of the wine and the water. Cover and poach for 12 minutes. Remove and drain (reserving the liquid). Keep warm.

3 Make a roux with the rest of the butter and the flour. Stir in about two-thirds of the reserved cooking liquid to make a sauce. Pour over the fish and vegetables. Sprinkle with parsley.

Serves 4

Sole Meunière

4 x 500 g (1–lb) whole soles, cleaned and skinned
50 g (2 oz) plain unbleached flour
1 tablespoon vegetable oil
100 g (3½ oz) unsalted butter
juice of ½ lemon, strained
sea salt and freshly ground black pepper
lemon wedges and sprigs of parsley, to garnish

1 Season the soles on both sides with salt and pepper, dredge in flour and shake off the excess.

2 Heat the oil and 25 g (1 oz) of the butter in a frying pan over high heat. Put 2 soles in the pan and sauté for 4 minutes on each side, until golden brown. Arrange on a serving dish and keep warm. Cook the other 2 soles in the same way.

3 Melt the remaining butter in the pan over medium heat, season and cook until nut-brown in colour. Remove from the heat and whisk in the lemon juice. Pour over the sole and serve garnished with lemon wedges and parsley.

Serves 4

Stuffed Plaice Fillets

8 fillets of plaice
175 ml (6 fl oz) vegetable stock or water
sprigs of tarragon, to garnish
FOR THE STUFFING:
175 g (6 oz) natural (undyed) smoked cod's roe
4 tablespoons fresh white breadcrumbs
juice of ½ lemon
freshly ground black pepper

1 Preheat the oven to Gas Mark 4/180°C/350°F. Put the cod's roe and breadcrumbs in a food processor and blend until smooth. Stir in the lemon juice and pepper.

2 Spread the stuffing along half the length of each plaice fillet and fold the other half over. Place in a buttered 25 cm (10–inch) square ovenproof dish and pour over the stock.

3 Cover and bake for 25 minutes. Remove the lid for the last 10 minutes of the cooking time. Serve garnished with sprigs of tarragon.

Serves 4

Plaice with Caper Sauce

8 fillets of plaice
600 ml (1 pint) court bouillon or fish stock
75 g (3 oz) unsalted butter
1 tablespoon lemon juice
1 tablespoon capers

1 Place 4 plaice fillets in a frying pan and pour over half of the court bouillon. Cover and poach over gentle heat for 8 minutes.

2 Remove the fish and arrange on a hot serving dish. Cover to keep warm. Cook the remaining fillets in the same way. Remove and keep warm. Pour away the court bouillon.

3 Melt the butter in the pan. When it is foaming, allow to brown slightly, and then remove the pan from the heat. Add the lemon juice and capers, and pour over the plaice. Serve immediately.

Serves 4

Prawn Vol au Vent

CONTRARY TO POPULAR BELIEF, A VOL AU VENT IS A LARGE PUFF PASTRY CASE FILLED WITH A SAVOURY SAUCE. SMALL PUFF PASTRY CASES ARE BOUCHEES (SEE THE VARIATIONS OVERLEAF).

SERVES 4

INGREDIENTS

175 g (6 oz) ready–made puff pastry, defrosted if frozen
beaten egg for glazing
lemon slices and mixed salad, to garnish
FOR THE FILLING:
500 g (1 lb) peeled prawns, defrosted if frozen
1 quantity of Parsley Sauce (page 55)
sea salt and freshly ground black pepper
lemon slices and mixed salad to serve

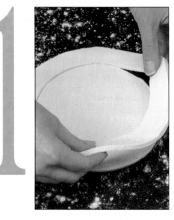

1 Preheat the oven to Gas Mark 6/ 200°C/400°F. Roll the dough out 6 mm (¹/4-inch) thick. Cut a 15-20 cm (6-8-inch) circle by cutting round a lid. Cut a smaller circle to make a ring, 2.5 cm (1-inch) wide. Lift off.

3 Bake for 10-15 minutes, until risen and golden. Lift out the risen centre and scoop out any uncooked dough. Dry the case out for a few minutes in a low oven.

2 Roll out the remaining circle the same diameter as the ring, and place on an oiled baking sheet. Dampen the edge and place the round on top. Mark it with a V pattern, prick the centre and glaze the edge with beaten egg.

4 Stir the prawns into the parsley sauce and season to taste. Fill the pastry case just before serving, either hot or cold. Garnish with sliced lemon and a mixed salad.

Tuna Bouchées

12 ready–made puff pastry small vol–au–vent cases
beaten egg or milk, for glazing
grated lemon zest and sprigs of dill and celery,
to garnish

FOR THE FILLING:
198 g can of tuna fish in brine
175 g (6 oz) curd cheese
pinch of ground mace
1 teaspoon grated lemon zest
2 celery sticks, chopped finely
sea salt and freshly ground black pepper

1 Preheat the oven to Gas Mark 6/200°C/400°F.
Place the pastry cases on a lightly oiled tray. Glaze
with egg or milk, and bake according to pack
instructions–usually about 10 minutes. Allow to
cool slightly.

2 Lift off the lids and scoop out any uncooked dough.
Flake the tuna into a mixing bowl and beat in the
cheese, mace and lemon zest. Stir in the celery and
season to taste.

3 Fill the cases and top with lemon zest. Serve hot or
cold, garnished with sprigs of dill and celery.

Serves 4

Kulebiaka

375 g (12 oz) ready–made puff pastry,
defrosted if frozen
125 g (4 oz) brown rice, cooked
2 tablespoons chopped parsley
2 free–range eggs, hard–boiled and chopped
500 g (1 lb) fresh salmon, cooked and flaked
sea salt and freshly ground black pepper
beaten egg, for glazing

1 Preheat the oven to Gas Mark 6/200°C/400°F.
Roll the pastry out to 50 x 30 cm (20 x 12 inches)
and place on an oiled baking sheet. Spread a
layer of rice over half of the pastry (the other half is
to be folded over).

2 Top the rice with half of both the parsley and the
chopped eggs followed by the salmon, the rest of
the parsley and egg and the remaining rice.
Season the layers to taste.

3 Fold over the pastry and seal the edges with
beaten egg, pinching to make a pattern. Cut some
leaves out of any pastry trimmings to decorate.
Brush with beaten egg, and bake for 30 minutes.

Serves 4

Salmon Puffs

2 large salmon steaks
250 g (8 oz) ready–made puff pastry,
defrosted if frozen
50 g (2 oz) shiitake mushrooms, diced
1 carrot, chopped
3 shallots, chopped
1 tablespoon olive oil
beaten egg or milk, for glazing

1 Preheat the oven to Gas Mark 4/180°C/350°F. Skin the salmon steaks and cut them in half, removing the bones. Fold each strip of salmon in half.

2 Roll out the pastry and cut out 4 x 10 cm (4–inch) squares. Place on an oiled baking sheet and put a salmon strip on each square. Run a lattice pastry cutter over the remaining pastry.

3 Gently fry the mushrooms, carrot and shallots in the oil until softened. Place a spoonful on top of the fish. Glaze the edges of the squares with the beaten egg or milk and top with the lattice pastry, sealing the edges. Bake for 25 minutes.

Serves 4

Trout en Croûte

375 g (12 oz) ready–made puff pastry,
defrosted if frozen
125 g (4 oz) shiitake mushrooms, chopped
2 carrots, chopped
25 g (1 oz) butter
2 large trout, filleted and skinned
sea salt and freshly ground black pepper
beaten egg, for glazing
4 black peppercorns

1 Preheat the oven to Gas Mark 6/200°C/400°F. Oil 2 baking trays. Roll out the pastry and cut out 8 fish–shaped pieces, each larger than the fillets. Place 2 on each baking sheet.

2 Gently fry the mushrooms and carrots in the butter for 10 minutes, until soft. Season and cool slightly. Place a trout fillet on top of each piece of pastry and top with the vegetable mixture.

3 Brush the edge of the pastry with beaten egg and top with the other pastry fish. Seal the edges and score scale marks on the fish. Put a smile on its face, add peppercorns for eyes and lightly brush with egg. Bake for 20 minutes.

Serves 4

Scallop and Bacon Kebabs

THE FAT IN THE BACON BASTES THE SCALLOPS AND KEEPS THEM MOIST
DURING COOKING. YOU CAN USE A VARIETY OF DIFFERENT FISH AND
SHELLFISH TO MAKE KEBABS, AS IN THE VARIATIONS OVERLEAF.

SERVES 2

INGREDIENTS

4 rashers back bacon, rind removed
1 medium head of broccoli, separated into florets
8 mange tout, trimmed and cut in half
8 scallops, cut in half
4 cherry tomatoes
1 tablespoon olive oil, for basting
boiled rice or pitta bread, to serve

not worth the fiddle

1 Flatten the bacon rashers by placing them on a chopping board and applying pressure with the flat blade of a palette knife until they are very thin. Cut them in half lengthways.

2 Blanch or steam the broccoli and mange tout until they are soft enough to be threaded onto a skewer, but not cooked. Drain and run under cold water to stop the cooking process.

3 Preheat the grill. Thread the broccoli, mange tout, scallops and cherry tomatoes on to the skewers, wrapping the bacon alternately under and over the scallops. Place under the hot grill.

4 Baste with olive oil and turn the kebabs frequently to ensure that they do not burn or dry out. Serve with rice or pitta and lots of green salad.

Courgette and Monkfish Brochettes

1 large courgette, cut into thin strips lengthways
250 g (8 oz) monkfish, boned and cubed
12 cherry tomatoes
12 small mushrooms, cut in half through the stalk
sprigs of basil, to garnish
FOR BASTING:
4 tablespoons olive oil
juice of 1 lemon

1 Blanch the courgette strips in boiling water for 2 minutes, or steam them until they are slightly soft and bendy.

2 Thread the courgette strips on to 4 skewers, alternating with pieces of fish, tomatoes and mushrooms.

3 Preheat the grill. Brush the brochettes with oil and lemon juice, and grill, turning frequently and basting, until the fish is cooked and golden. Serve garnished with sprigs of basil.

Serves 2

Tandoori Tiger Prawn Kebabs

150 g (5 oz) natural yogurt
2 teaspoons garam masala
pinch of chilli powder (cayenne)
8 large uncooked tiger prawns
1 red pepper, seeded and cut into squares
1 green pepper, seeded and cut into squares
lemon wedges, to serve

1 Mix the yogurt with the spices and marinate the prawns in the spicy mixture for at least 2 hours. Remove the prawns and reserve the marinade.

2 Blanch the peppers in boiling water, or cook them, covered, in a microwave oven on full power for 2 minutes, until they are softened and partially cooked.

3 Preheat the grill. Thread the prawns and peppers on to 4 skewers and place under the grill, turning frequently and basting with the reserved marinade, until the prawns have turned pink and are cooked. Serve garnished with lemon wedges.

Serves 2

Shish Fish Kebab

2 medium mackerel fillets, skinned
250 g (8 oz) coley fillet, skinned
1 teaspoon ground cumin
1 teaspoon ground coriander
¼ teaspoon ground turmeric
1 tablespoon tomato purée
salad leaves and lemon wedges, to garnish

1 Place the mackerel and coley fillets with the spices and tomato purée in a food processor or blender and blend to a smooth purée.

2 Working carefully, using floured hands, divide the mixture equally into 4 portions and form around 4 skewers.

3 Preheat the grill. Place the kebabs on an oiled or buttered sheet of cooking foil under the grill and cook for 5 minutes on each side, turning carefully. Serve on a bed of salad leaves, garnished with lemon wedges.

Serves 2

Oyster and Prune Kebabs

125 g (4 oz) shiitake mushrooms, sliced
½ tablespoon olive oil
12 oysters in their shells
8 prunes, pitted and cooked or ready-to-eat
12 cherry tomatoes
1 courgette, sliced into rounds
FOR BASTING:
juice of ½ lemon
3 tablespoons olive oil

1 Gently fry the mushrooms in the olive oil until lightly cooked. Remove from the pan and drain on absorbent kitchen paper.

2 Hold each oyster, rounded shell up, over a strainer in a bowl to catch the juice. Insert the tip of a short sharp blade into the hinge and twist the knife to prise it apart. Run the blade between the shells and cut away the oyster. Reserve the juices.

3 Preheat the grill. Thread the mushrooms, oysters, prunes, tomatoes and courgette on to 4 skewers, alternating in a uniform pattern. Place under the grill and cook, basting with lemon juice and oil, and turning occasionally. Spoon the oyster juice over the kebabs just before serving.

Serves 2

Seafood Salad

THIS SALAD WILL APPEAL TO EVERYONE WHO LOVES MIXED SEAFOOD
DISHES THAT EVOKE THE FLAVOURS OF THE MEDITERRANEAN. AS
PREPARATION IS TIME-CONSUMING, USE THIS DISH FOR SPECIAL OCCASIONS.

SERVES 4

INGREDIENTS

1 kg (2 lb) fresh mussels in their shells,
  scrubbed and cleaned (page 42)
1 red pepper, seeded and halved
1 yellow pepper, seeded and halved
2 tablespoons olive oil
2 teaspoons balsamic vinegar
500 g (1 lb) cooked prawns in their shells
1 bag of mixed washed salad leaves

2 tablespoons chopped basil
sprigs of basil, to garnish
FOR THE DRESSING:
4 tablespoons olive oil
1 tablespoon lemon juice
1 teaspoon Dijon mustard
sea salt and freshly ground black pepper

Discard any damaged mussels and those that remain open when tapped. Cook them in 150 ml (¹/4 pint) water for 5 minutes, until they open. Drain and discard any that remain closed and remove from the shells.

Peel the prawns (reserving 8 in their shells for decoration). Put all the dressing ingredients in a screw-top jar and shake until well blended. Toss the mussels and prawns together in the dressing.

Preheat the grill. Flatten the pepper halves and place, skin-side up, under the grill until charred. Remove and, when they are cool enough to handle, skin them and cut into strips. Place in the oil and vinegar.

Arrange the salad leaves in a serving dish and toss in the pepper strips and basil. Top with the mussels and prawns, and garnish with the reserved prawns in their shells and the sprigs of basil.

Salad Nicoise

500 g (1 lb) small waxy salad potatoes,
scraped and halved
2 lettuce hearts, one crispy, one soft leaved
200 g can of tuna fish, drained and flaked
4 free–range eggs, hard–boiled and quartered
50 g (2 oz) anchovy fillets, drained
175 g (6 oz) thin green beans, cooked
4 plum tomatoes, skinned and quartered
75 g (3 oz) black olives
FOR THE VINAIGRETTE:
150 ml (¼ pint) extra–virgin olive oil
1 garlic clove, crushed
4 tablespoons red wine vinegar
1 heaped teaspoon Dijon mustard
2 tablespoons chopped mixed herbs

1 Boil the potatoes until just cooked. Drain. Put all the vinaigrette ingredients in a screw–top jar and shake well. Pour half over the warm potatoes.

2 Arrange the lettuce leaves in a salad dish. Place the tuna in the centre and top with some of the egg quarters and half of the anchovies.

3 Toss the potatoes, beans and tomatoes in the remaining dressing and arrange around the tuna and egg. Put the remaining egg quarters on top, and scatter with olives and anchovy fillets.

Serves 4

Smoked Mackerel Salad

1 heart of medium–sized frisee lettuce
1 small head of radicchio
1 small pack of lambs' lettuce or rocket
2 thick stalks celery, chopped
⅓ cucumber, chopped
4 smoked mackerel fillets
sea salt and freshly ground black pepper
1 lemon, cut into 8 wedges, to serve
FOR THE DRESSING:
3 tablespoons mayonnaise
2 teaspoons horseradish sauce
sea salt and freshly ground black pepper

1 Wash and thoroughly dry the salad leaves. Tear and toss together in the base of a large salad bowl. Scatter over the celery and cucumber, and season with salt and pepper.

2 Skin the mackerel fillets and carefully slice them in half vertically. Cut into chunks, and arrange on top of the salad.

3 Combine the dressing ingredients until well blended and offer separately. Serve with the lemon wedges.

Serves 4

Californian Sea Bass Salad

2 sea bass, cleaned and filleted
olive oil for basting
1 ciabatta loaf with olives
salad leaves or watercress
freshly ground black pepper
FOR THE SALSA:
250 g (8 oz) tomatoes, skinned, seeded
and chopped
½ onion, chopped
2 tablespoons olive oil
2 teaspoons sherry vinegar
1 red pepper, roasted or grilled and skin removed
few drops of Tabasco (hot pepper) sauce
sea salt and freshly ground black pepper

1 Place all the salsa ingredients in a food processor or blender, and blend until roughly chopped. Set aside while you cook the fish.

2 Brush the sea bass with olive oil and cook on a hot griddle for about 5 minutes. Turn the fillets once for cross-hatch marking. Alternatively, grill them.

3 Cut the ciabatta loaf in half horizontally. Quarter and brush with olive oil. Toast the cut side under a preheated grill. Place the fish on top and serve with the salad and salsa. Drizzle over a little extra olive oil and sprinkle with black pepper.

Serves 4

Curried Fish Salad

250 g (8 oz) salmon
1 trout, cleaned
1 bag of mixed salad leaves
12 cherry tomatoes
2 free-range eggs, hard-boiled, shelled and
quartered
snipped chives, to garnish
FOR THE DRESSING:
½ teaspoon ground coriander
½ teaspoon ground cumin
¼ teaspoon ground turmeric
4 tablespoons greek-style natural yogurt or
double cream

1 Preheat the grill and place the salmon and trout under it. Grill until cooked, turning half-way through. Remove from the heat and, when cool enough to handle, flake the fish from the skin and bones.

2 Mix together the salad dressing ingredients and toss the salmon and trout gently in the dressing.

3 Toss the salad leaves with the tomatoes and arrange in a serving dish. Put the fish in the centre and garnish with the egg and snipped chives.

Serves 4

Finnan Haddock Flan

SMOKED FISH GIVES A GOOD FLAVOUR TO FLANS AND QUICHES AS IN THIS
DELICIOUS RECIPE. ON THE FOLLOWING PAGES THERE ARE SOME
INTERESTING VARIATIONS ON THIS THEME, USING FISH AND SHELLFISH.

SERVES 4

INGREDIENTS

175 g (6 oz) ready–made shortcrust pastry
FOR THE FILLING:
300 g (10 oz) Finnan haddock or other smoked haddock
150 ml (¼ pint) single cream OR full-fat milk
2 free–range eggs
1 tablespoon chopped parsley
2 tomatoes, halved
freshly ground black pepper
parsley sprigs, to garnish

1 *Preheat the oven to Gas Mark 6/ 200°C/400°F. Line a lightly oiled 20 cm (8-inch) flan tin with the pastry. Line the pastry case with greaseproof paper and baking beans and 'bake blind' for 10 minutes.*

3 *Beat together the cream (or milk), eggs, pepper and parsley, and pour over the fish. Place the tomato halves in position, marking out quarters in the flan.*

2 *Poach the haddock in enough cold water to cover for about 10 minutes, until the fish is cooked. When it is cool enough to handle, flake the flesh into the base of the pastry case.*

4 *Lower the oven temperature to Gas Mark 5/190°C/ 375°F, and bake the flan for 25-30 minutes. When golden brown and set, remove from the oven and cool on a wire baking tray. Serve in wedges, garnished with parsley sprigs.*

Seafood Tartlets

175 g (6 oz) ready-made shortcrust pastry
FOR THE FILLING:
150 g (5 oz) natural yogurt
2 free-range eggs, beaten lightly
6 tablespoons double cream
2 teaspoons whole red peppercorns, crushed
125 g (4 oz) peeled cooked prawns
150 g (5 oz) salmon fillet or steak, skinned and cut into chunks
sea salt (and freshly ground black pepper, if liked)

1 Preheat the oven to Gas Mark 6/200°C/400°F. Line 4 large or 8 small lightly oiled tartlet tins with the pastry. Alternatively, line a 20 cm (8-inch) flan tin and 'bake blind' (page 88).

2 Combine the yogurt, eggs and cream. Season and stir in the peppercorns.

3 Place the prawns and salmon in the base of the prepared pastry case(s), and pour in the egg mixture. Bake until set and golden in colour.

Serves 4

Tuna Quiche

175 g (6 oz) ready-made shortcrust pastry
FOR THE FILLING:
150 ml (¼ pint) single cream
2 free-range eggs
198 g can of tuna fish in oil, drained and flaked
198 g can of sweetcorn kernels, drained, if necessary
1 tablespoon chopped chives
sea salt and freshly ground black pepper
snipped chives, to garnish

1 Preheat the oven to Gas Mark 6/200°C/400°F. Line a lightly oiled 20 cm (8-inch) flan tin with the pastry. Line the pastry case with greaseproof paper and baking beans and 'bake blind' for 10 minutes (page 88).

2 Beat together the cream, eggs and seasoning, and mix with the tuna, sweetcorn and chives.

3 Pour the filling into the pastry case. Lower the oven temperature to Gas Mark 5/190°C/375°F, and bake for 25-30 minutes, until set and golden. Serve garnished with snipped chives.

Serves 4

Crab Flan

175 g (6 oz) ready–made shortcrust pastry
25g (1 oz) grated parmesan cheese
snipped chives, to garnish
FOR THE FILLING:
3 free–range eggs
150 ml (¼ pint) single cream
3 shakes of Worcestershire sauce
1 dressed crab
freshly ground black pepper
chilli powder (cayenne) for dusting

1 Preheat the oven to Gas Mark 6/200°C/400°F. Roll out the pastry, adding the parmesan cheese, and use to line a lightly oiled 20 cm (8–inch) flan tin. Line the pastry case with greaseproof paper and baking beans and 'bake blind' for 10 minutes (page 88).

2 Beat together the eggs, cream, Worcestershire sauce and seasoning, and stir in the crabmeat. Pour into the pastry case and dust the top with cayenne pepper.

3 Lower the oven temperature to Gas Mark 5/ 190°C/375°F and bake the flan for 25–30 minutes, until set and golden brown. Serve cut into wedges, sprinkled with chives.

Serves 4

Pissaladière

175 g (6 oz) ready–made shortcrust pastry
pinch of ground cinnamon
FOR THE TOPPING:
625 g (1¼ lb) onions, chopped
2 garlic cloves, crushed
4 tablespoons olive oil
400 g can of chopped tomatoes
2 tablespoons tomato purée
2 teaspoons thyme leaves
75 g (3 oz) black olives
2 x 50 g cans of anchovies, drained
sea salt and freshly ground black pepper

1 Preheat the oven to Gas Mark 6/200°C/400°F. Roll out the pastry, working in the cinnamon, and use to line a lightly oiled shallow 20 cm (8–inch) flan tin. Line the pastry case with greaseproof paper and beans, and 'bake blind' for 15 minutes (page 88).

2 Gently fry the onions and garlic in the olive oil for 7 minutes. Add the tomatoes, tomato purée and thyme, and simmer for 15 minutes. Season.

3 Spread the tomato mixture over the pastry base. Arrange the olives and anchovies over the top, and heat through in the oven for about 10 minutes.

Serves 4

Seafood Lasagne

In this variation on the classic Italian pasta dish, the layers of smooth white sauce and light plaice contrast well with the spicier and more colourful scallop and tomato sauce.

Serves 4

INGREDIENTS

175 g (6 oz) pre–cooked green or white lasagne (fresh or dried)
1 tablespoon coarsely grated parmesan cheese

FOR THE WHITE SAUCE:
25 g (1 oz) butter or soft margarine
25 g (1 oz) plain unbleached flour
450 ml (¾ pint) skimmed milk

3 skinned plaice fillets, sliced
2 tablespoons chopped parsley

FOR THE SCALLOP SAUCE:
2 garlic cloves, crushed
2 tablespoons olive oil
8 scallops
397 g can of tomatoes, chopped roughly
sea salt and freshly ground black pepper

1 Preheat the oven to Gas Mark 5/ 190 °C/375 °F. Make the white sauce: melt the butter and stir in the flour to make a roux. Gradually stir in the milk to make a smooth sauce.

3 Gently fry the garlic in the oil and stir in the scallops and tomatoes. Continue to cook for 5 minutes. Season to taste. Place half of the scallop sauce on top of the lasagne in the dish.

2 Stir in the plaice and parsley, and pour half of the sauce into a lightly oiled 20 cm (8-inch) square ovenproof dish. Cover with a layer of lasagne.

4 Continue layering up in this way with the pasta and sauces, finishing with white sauce. Sprinkle with parmesan, cover with foil and bake for 25 minutes. Remove the foil for the last 10 minutes to brown the top.

BALANCE

Pasta with Spicy Mussel Sauce

½ onion, chopped
1 garlic clove, crushed
1 red chilli, seeded and chopped
1 tablespoon thyme leaves
6 halves of sun–dried tomatoes, chopped
1 tablespoon of oil from the sun–dried tomatoes
397 g can of chopped tomatoes
500 g (1 lb) fresh mussels in their shells, scrubbed
and cleaned (page 42)
250 g (8 oz) pasta, e.g. penne (quills) or
conchiglie (shells)
chopped parsley, to garnish

1 Lightly fry the onion, garlic, chilli, thyme and sun–dried tomatoes in the oil for 10 minutes. Add the chopped tomatoes and continue to cook for 15 minutes, until reduced and thickened.

2 Purée in a blender or food processor. Return to the saucepan. Cook the mussels separately as per step 1 of Moules Pescatora (page 44). Discard any mussels that fail to open. Stir the rest into the sauce.

3 Meanwhile, cook the pasta in plenty of lightly salted, boiling water for about 12 minutes until tender but still firm. Drain and toss with the sauce. Serve sprinkled with parsley.

Serves 4

Spaghetti Vongole

250 ml (8 fl oz) olive oil
3 garlic cloves, chopped
1 green chilli, seeded and chopped
1 tablespoon chopped parsley
750 g (1½ lb) ripe plum tomatoes, skinned and
chopped finely
1 kg (2 lb) fresh clams in their shells OR 2 x 290 g
cans of clams, drained
250 g (8 oz) spaghetti
sea salt and freshly ground black pepper

1 Heat the olive oil and add the garlic, chilli and parsley, and cook for 2 minutes. Add the chopped tomatoes and cook for 15 minutes.

2 Add the fresh clams and cook for 5 minutes, until the shells have opened. If using canned clams, stir gently into the tomato mixture and heat through. Season to taste.

3 While the sauce is cooking, cook the spaghetti in plenty of lightly salted, boiling water until cooked but still *al dente* (offering some resistance when bitten). Toss the sauce and pasta together, and serve immediately.

Serves 4

Cullen Skink 4-6

{ 2 smoked Haddock Fillets (1lb app) Skinned
{ 1 either non smoked or another smoked one.

1 pt milk
2 bay leaves
3 med leeks/onions
3oz butter
9oz pot cubed.
1 tbsp flr.
1-2 tsp mustard pdr.
1 tsp sugar
4.5 tbsp dbl cream
2 tbsp chopped parsley

1/ Fish into pan with milk. Bring to simmering pt. Turn off.
2/ Chop leeks(or onions) include green (using leeks not coarse tops)
3/ melt Butter fry leeks 5 mins Don't brown.
4/ Add pots + cup H₂O. Bring to boil Simmer 5-8 mins until H₂O evaporated.
5/ Stir in Flour cook 1 minute

6/ Drain Fish. Save milk.
7/ Slowly add milk to vegetable pan Stirring until a soupy consistency reached
8/ Simmer for few mins until Pots cooked but not mushy
9/ Mix Mustard Pdr with 1 tbsp H₂O
10/ Stir into Soup
11/ flake fish (no bones)
12/ Add to Soup with sugar
13/ Add cream + parsley
14/ Season Stir Serve.

telegraph.co.uk/bestbritishrecipes

Cod Cannelloni

12 cannelloni tubes
grated parmesan cheese, to serve
FOR THE CANNELLONI FILLING:
1 yellow pepper, seeded and chopped
2 garlic cloves, crushed
1 tablespoon vegetable oil
500 g (1 lb) cod fillet, skinned and minced
1 tablespoon chopped parsley
FOR THE SAUCE:
½ onion, chopped
1 garlic clove, crushed
pinch of chilli powder (cayenne)
1 tablespoon olive oil
2 x 398 g cans of chopped tomatoes
sea salt and freshly ground black pepper

1 Preheat the oven to Gas Mark 4/180°C/350°F. Gently fry the pepper and garlic in the oil. Season and stir in the cod and parsley. Cook for 3 minutes. Use to fill the cannelloni tubes.

2 Gently fry the onion, garlic and chilli in the oil. Season and stir in the tomatoes. Cook for 10 minutes, and then liquidize to a smooth sauce.

3 Place some sauce in an ovenproof dish. Layer the cannelloni and sauce. Cover and cook for 25–30 minutes. Serve sprinkled with parmesan.

Serves 4 *Boring. Needs jazzing up 2nd time did jazz up - Still boring!*

Pasta with Seafood Sauce

2 garlic cloves, crushed
1 large onion, chopped
2 green peppers, seeded and chopped
2 tablespoons olive oil
500 g (1 lb) tomatoes, chopped
250 g (8 oz) shelled cooked mussels
250 g (8 oz) peeled cooked prawns,
50 g can of anchovies, drained
1 tablespoon capers
1 carrot, peeled and grated
250 g (8 oz) tortellini or pasta of your choice
grated parmesan cheese, to serve

1 Gently fry the garlic, onion and peppers in the oil until softened, but not browned. Add the tomatoes and cook for about 15 minutes, stirring occasionally, until a thick sauce has formed.

2 Stir in the mussels, prawns, anchovies and capers and heat through. Just before serving, stir in the carrot, leaving it crunchy in texture.

3 Meanwhile, cook the pasta in plenty of lightly salted, boiling water until cooked but still *al dente* (offering some resistance when bitten). Toss the sauce and pasta together. Serve with grated parmesan cheese.

Serves 4

Index